9·25·79

YOUR FUTURE AS A LEGAL ASSISTANT

YOUR FUTURE
AS A LEGAL ASSISTANT

By

CHARLES D. HEATH

RICHARDS ROSEN PRESS, INC.
New York, New York 10010

Published in 1979 by Richards Rosen Press, Inc.
29 East 21st Street, New York, N.Y. 10010

FIRST EDITION

Library of Congress Cataloging in Publication Data

Heath, Charles Dickinson, 1941–
    Your future as a legal assistant.

    (Careers in depth)
    1. Legal assistants—United States. 2. Laws—
Vocational guidance—United States. I. Title.
KF320.L4H4   340′.023   78–10516
ISBN 0–8239–0477–6

Manufactured in the United States of America

About the Author

Charles D. Heath is a member of the State Bars of Wisconsin and Arizona, the American Bar Association, and the Sheboygan County (Wisconsin) Bar Association. He has also been admitted to practice law before the Supreme Courts of Indiana, Iowa, and Pennsylvania and is licensed to practice law before the Supreme Court of the United States. His principal interest is in the field of corporate and business law. He is currently Assistant General Counsel, Kohler Co., Kohler, Wisconsin, a major manufacturer of  plumbing products, engines, and generator sets for residential, commercial, and industrial applications.

Mr. Heath holds a Bachelor of Business Administration degree, which was awarded with distinction from the University of Iowa, and is a graduate of that university's College of Law, where he was a member of the Board of Editors of the *Iowa Law Review*. He also holds a Master of Business Administration degree from the University of Arizona at Tucson. He was selected to join Beta Gamma Sigma, the national scholastic honorary society in business administration, both as an undergraduate and a graduate student.

From 1973 Mr. Heath has assisted in establishing the Legal Assistant Course Program at Lakeshore Technical Institute,

Cleveland, Wiconsin. He served as Chairman of the original Ad Hoc Legal Assistant Course Program Advisory Committee and as a member of subsequent advisory committees; instructor of the legal-technical courses in Domestic Relations and Introduction to Corporate Law Practice; part-time coordinator of the Legal Assistant Course Program at Lakeshore Technical Institute; and a member of the Wisconsin State Board—Vocational, Technical and Adult Education—Committee on Legal Assistants responsible for approving the establishment of additional Legal Assistant course programs within the vocational, technical, and adult education system in Wisconsin.

Acknowledgments

Many thanks are due to the administration and staff and past and present members of the Ad Hoc and Permanent Legal Assistant Advisory Committee, Lakeshore Technical Institute, Cleveland, Wisconsin.

Special thanks go to the Standing Committee on Legal Assistants of the American Bar Association; the National Association of Legal Assistants, Inc.; and the National Federation of Paralegal Associations for permission to reprint certain copyrighted and uncopyrighted material.

Contents

Introduction

What is a legal assistant? What do legal assistants do each day, for what purpose? Does a legal assistant do the same things each day? Does every legal assistant do the same things as every other legal assistant? Is a legal assistant's career as glamorous as the name implies? What is meant by the legal services *team?* Will those who seek to enter a legal assistant's career find job satisfaction and financial reward?

Those women[1] and men who work as legal assistants[2] "under the supervision of a lawyer . . . apply knowledge of law and legal procedures, techniques, services, and processes, prepare and interpret legal documents; detail procedures for practicing in certain fields of law; research, select, assess, compile, and use information from the law library and other references; and analyze and handle procedural problems that involve independent decisions."[3]

Legal assistants have counterparts in the fields of medicine and dentistry. Medical assistants are trained to perform necessary

---

[1] Throughout this book, the reader should keep in mind that "she" or "woman" may refer to persons of either sex. Both women and men have an equal right to make careers as legal assistants, and that thought is emphasized here. A current examination of the field as a whole, however, reveals that more women than men are present.

[2] Other names for this occupation include paralegal; paraprofessional or legal paraprofessional; paralegal assistant; attorney's or lawyer's assistant; legal technician or certified legal technician; and lay assistant, lay advocate, or nonlawyer advocate. Generally, the term legal assistant will be used in this book. In particular circumstances—for example, proper names or quotations—other names, especially paralegal, may be used.

[3] From the definition of a legal assistant by the National Association of Legal Assistants, Inc., Tulsa, Oklahoma.

but repetitive clinical procedures or administrative tasks. Paramedics, unlike medical assistants, are usually thought of as performing emergency procedures or providing basic medical treatment before transportation to a hospital or a doctor's care, and thus they have no direct counterparts in the legal assistant field. Medical assistants, on the other hand, whether clinical or administrative, are usually viewed like legal assistants as office personnel.

Likewise, dental assistants or dental hygienists help dentists in ways similar to those in which medical assistants help doctors.

As recently as 1973, *Webster's New Collegiate Dictionary* did not list either the term "legal assistant" or the word "paralegal." Nevertheless, parameters of the profession have been described and will be discussed here. This discussion will be in terms of who the legal assistant is and is not and what the legal assistant does or may do and does not or may not do. A legal assistant is not a lawyer and properly not a person such as a law student who intends to become a lawyer. Generally, a law student working in a law office or in a legally related activity during summer vacations or during the school year before graduation from law school or immediately thereafter while awaiting admission to the practice of law is referred to as a law clerk and not a legal assistant. Law clerking is usually considered one step in the educational process aimed at graduation from law school and admission to the bar and not as an end in itself. On the other hand, the field of legal assistant is becoming an increasingly recognized occupational goal.

The greatest conceptual blur appears to occur between the occupational roles of a legal assistant and a legal secretary. A legal assistant may once have been but, as a legal assistant, is not a legal secretary. A legal assistant may never have been a legal secretary. The legal assistant may be able to type, file, and make appointments; however, if and to the extent that these activities are done, they are incidental functions and not fundamental job tasks.

Legal assistants, like lawyers, are involved with the law. Legal assistants help lawyers with necessary and interesting jobs, some-times involving direct contact with clients. Examples of ways in which legal assistants help lawyers include obtaining informa-tion by interviewing clients or otherwise; preparing or assisting in the preparation of legal documents on the basis of informa-tion obtained; and having legal documents thus prepared filed with the appropriate office or offices.

The lawyer, the legal assistant, and the legal secretary all are important members of the legal services *team*. Each team mem-ber has a different but important part to play. Provided each plays his part well, the results achieved by the team should be greater than those obtainable by any single member of the team. This is the concept of synergism. The team will be most likely to obtain synergism if each member performs those tasks for which he or she is best suited.

It has been said that the tasks of the lawyer are three in number: (1) to obtain the facts; (2) to research the law; and (3) to apply the law to the facts in order to reach a legal con-clusion. Simply stated, the lawyer gives legal advice or counsels or represents clients. As we shall learn later in this introductory chapter, ethical considerations prohibit the legal assistant from giving legal advice or counseling or representing clients. Never-theless, to the extent that the legal assistant can relieve the lawyer from having to determine the facts or research the law, the lawyer can then concentrate on that third task which only he or she can do. The clerical tasks of the legal secretary are in-numerable. Typing, filing, and making appointments are merely examples. Perhaps the principal task of the legal secretary is maintaining an orderly flow of work.

What the legal assistant may do is subject to certain conditions and limitations, both ethical and practical. Ethically, the legal assistant may not consult with nor advise clients. In addition, the legal assistant may not represent clients in court or before an administrative agency, except perhaps under very limited cir-cumstances. All activities and actions of the legal assistant are subject to the supervision of the employing lawyer. Should the legal assistant make an error, he or she is, of course, responsible. But the employing lawyer is also responsible.

Practically, legal assistants should not presume to be able to do more than they have been trained or acquired the experience to do, whether through formal or on-the-job instruction. The legal assistant, therefore, will concentrate on duties that are already routine or are capable of being made routine, while exercising judgment on which matters are routine or capable of being made routine and which are not. As the knowledge and skill of the legal assistant grow, he or she can help the lawyer on matters of increasing complexity. In this way the legal assistant enables the lawyer to spend more time advising or consulting with clients and representing their interests and increases the synergism of the legal services team.

Variety and interest in performing the job of legal assistant are created by the addition of client contact. No one client is like any other, even though the problems of each may be similar. Variety and interest are also added by the vast array of legal subjects, for the same fields of law are available for possible employment of legal assistants as are available to lawyers themselves. These varied fields cover the alphabet from Appellate Practice to Zoning; from clients who say: "I'll take my case all the way to the Supreme Court of the United States, if necessary," to those who query: "My neighbor can't put a hot dog stand next to my house, can he?" In between appellate practice and zoning lie, for example, estate planning, personal injury, and trial preparation.

Another element of variety and interest is provided by the type of law practice. There are lawyers who specialize by particular field of law, such as criminal law or labor law. These lawyers usually are in the big cities, working for major companies or the federal government. In addition to specialists, there are lawyers who engage in the general practice of law. General practitioners often work in small cities and towns and rural areas. These lawyers serve the family on legal matters much as the family doctor looks after Mom, Dad, and the kids for complaints ranging from those treated with aspirin and bed rest to conditions of zymotic disease.

Opportunities exist for legal assistants in business and industry, in all branches of government—legislative, executive, and judicial—and at all levels, local, state, and federal. Of course, the largest employers of legal assistants are lawyers engaged in the private practice of law, whether as general practitioners or specialists.

As indicated in the discussion of other members of the legal services team, law-related careers other than legal assistant are also possible. Careers are available as legal administrators, who use business administration skills to manage the law office. A career as a law librarian is a special library career. Attorneys often employ investigators to assist them in gathering facts, particularly in criminal law practice, in domestic relations cases, and in preparation for personal injury litigation. The smaller the law office, the more likely it is that the functions of legal assistant, legal secretary, legal administrator, law librarian, and investigator will be performed by one and the same person. As the size of the law office increases, the unique functions performed by each will become increasingly clear, and two or more persons will likely be employed to perform them.

Good luck in your chosen occupation, whether or not it be the field of legal assistant or a law-related career.

YOUR FUTURE AS A LEGAL ASSISTANT

CHAPTER I

The Personality and Abilities Necessary for a Legal Assistant Career

You, like all of us, will at various times throughout your life suffer defeat and disappointment, for human tragedy comes in a never-ending variety of forms. Over some of this misfortune, you will have no control. Some of this unhappiness, however, you will bring upon yourself through bad decision-making. Perhaps the most important choice you will make during your life is the selection of a mate. Certainly a close second in importance is the career you will choose. In the choice of a mate it is sometimes said that "Opposites attract," and a marriage of opposites is one possible kind of successful marriage. Unfortunately, a career decision generally does not allow for that possibility. A career that will bring job satisfaction and personal happiness is one in which personality and abilities are closely matched to the career choice. Without the proper alignment of personality and abilities with career, the fact that a wrong decision has been made will be discovered sooner or later. Of course, the sooner such a discovery is made, the better for you it will be. At worst, after the investment of effort, time, and money, and with that famous 20–20 hindsight, you may find that the choice of a career as a legal assistant was the wrong one for you. Even if the discovery is made after you have become employed as a legal assistant, it is better to move on to another career that will afford the chance for job satisfaction and personal happiness than to stay and suffer in silence for the rest of your working life. How much better it would be if that discovery could be made before training is begun. For these reasons, it is highly desirable that you read and study this chapter on personality and abilities with the intention of developing the foresight to know that the choice of a career as a legal assistant is the right one for you before you begin your training.

You may wonder why such a study is important when the field of law is so vast that it affects all of us most of the time. Surely, you may think, you will be able to find your place somewhere, if not as a generalist, then in one of the many specialized fields of law.

A variety of positions are available, both general and specialized. This variety does allow for a great deal of matching of individual personalities and abilities with jobs. But, as many would-be lawyers have found, it is unwise to enter a field if its personal as well as other demands cannot be met. You will have a far better chance for success as a legal assistant if you are well qualified as a person for such a career. For example, if you are generally speaking easily frustrated, you are undoubtedly more likely to find job satisfaction and personal happiness in some other career field.

With these thoughts in mind, let us probe more deeply into your personality and abilities, paying particular attention to those characteristics that make you unique in all the world.

Individual characteristics of personality and ability are so complex and great in number that it is hard to know where to begin. Let us rank as the most important personal trait the one that has already been mentioned. In working as a legal assistant, frustration may arise to the extent that certain tasks must be repeated time and again, sometimes even for the same client. For the legal assistant, patience is a virtue of the highest order. Although it is difficult to say which personal qualities are more important than others, the legal assistant must also be willing to "take a back seat" to the lawyer-employer and to the client they both serve. To a certain extent, the legal assistant is in the position of serving two masters. When the wishes of the client and the employer conflict, the legal assistant must have the ability to be a bit of a diplomat, while recognizing that his or her employer is the lawyer and not the client. Third, the legal assistant must be willing to take and follow orders given by the lawyer. Fourth, the legal assistant must be a self-starter, and self-sustaining and self-sufficient once he or she gets started.

Will you be a participant, or only an observer? Will you get involved in making the world a better place in which to live? Or will your frustration only be increased by shifting your attention from the problems of individual clients to the elimination of the factors that may be causing those problems?

Some believe that many men and women who train to become legal assistants may have difficulty in obtaining employment. Will you be willing both to compete and to compromise? For example, law school graduates themselves are currently competing for jobs in a very crowded market. According to one 1976 source,[1] for every three law school graduates, only two will find jobs. In 1974, 30,000 students received law degrees, almost three times the level of 1963. More than half of this increase occurred between 1971 and 1974. The prospect of 10,000 more law school graduates than jobs is expected to continue into the 1980's as the result of more and more law schools graduating larger and larger classes. A downturn in the national economy will likely only make the problem greater.

Looking at how this circumstance may affect employment opportunities for legal assistants, it has been said:

"The problem for law students is that many of the jobs they perform in the summer for law firms are now being done by paralegals. Eventually, paralegals may do the work that many

---

[1] Locin, Mitchell, "Law graduates competing for jobs in crowded market," Chicago *Tribune,* Sunday, May 16, 1976, p. 33.

beginning lawyers do, further damaging the prospects for a law school graduate to find a job."[2]

In other words, the legal assistant must be competitive, perhaps highly competitive. Not only may he or she be competing for jobs with other legal assistants, but also for jobs with recent law school graduates. Will you take up the battle for a job after you have spent the effort, time, and money to qualify as a legal assistant? Will you be willing to accept the employment that is available even though it may not be precisely what you wanted? If necessary, will you be willing to accept a smaller financial reward than that to which you feel entitled by your ability and training? In other words, do you have that important personal trait of flexibility?

The existence of the legal services team of the lawyer, the legal assistant, and the legal secretary was mentioned earlier. You may have guessed that the growth of the legal assistant field is likely to lead to an increasing emphasis on the team approach. If you do not like working closely with people, a career as a legal assistant is not for you. In this connection, will you get along well with other members of the team as well as with clients? Can you rapidly and readily become involved with clients and their problems? Can you understand their wants, concerns, and difficulties? Can you recognize that people react as they do for a reason? Will you take the time where necessary to seek out the reason and try to be understanding and sympathetic? Are you willing to accept the proposition, as a simple variation on a familiar theme, that: "You can please some of the people all of the time and all of the people some of the time; but you can't please all of the people all of the time"? Will your acceptance of that proposition extend to your relationship with your employer? Moreover, can you accept criticism, whether or not you believe it is justified?

Once you have received your training and become employed, will you exert the effort to maintain your competence as a legal

---

[2] Locin, Mitchell, "Paralegal laymen move into field," Chicago *Tribune*, Sunday, May 16, 1976, p. 33.

assistant? Will you read and attend lectures and engage in a general program of continuing education through an educational institution or association or club of legal assistants?

In summary, your personality, your traits, and your characteristics, as they impact on the remaining members of the legal services team, clients, and others, are of major importance. Unfortunately, you will not be able to travel the road to a successful career as a legal assistant on personality alone. Some education or training beyond high school will be a necessity if you choose a career as a legal assistant. A minimum of two years of education or training beyond high school will be required. As many as four years or more may be appropriate compared to the seven years of education required of lawyers.

CHAPTER II

High School and Beyond

Whether a four-year business administration or liberal arts degree is necessary or even desirable for those seeking careers as legal assistants is the subject of possible debate. However, more responsible and better paying positions in particular legal assistant specialties in larger cities may be available to those who obtain a general college education before or while training as legal assistants. The cost of four or more years of education is a factor to be considered. Another factor is the income you could be earning as a practicing legal assistant that a period of education beyond the necessary minimum will require you to forgo. Today four years of college before training as a legal assistant may simply reflect a decision or realization that four years of education beyond high school has not prepared the graduate for any particular career. On the other hand, four years of college while training as a legal assistant may represent a conscious choice to aim for those more responsible and better paying positions previously mentioned.

In any event, if you begin to plan a career as a legal assistant while still in high school, you should organize your courses accordingly, as well as both planned extracurricular activity or activities and what would otherwise be free time.

What we say now, then, would apply to all of you who would seek a career as a legal assistant. Become familiar with the rest of this chapter whatever your present circumstances, whether your high school education is continuing or has been completed and whether your current plans include four years of college or not.

It is particularly important for the person who desires a legal assistant career to take the college preparatory course. This is true even though it may appear that time or cost or the forgone income will preclude attending four years of college. The intellectual stimulation of association with students who do contemplate a college education is valuable whether or not that particular objective is obtained. While still in high school, you should emphasize English and related courses such as foreign languages and speech. Include those languages which, like English, are derived from Latin. These include, for example, French and Spanish. Try a course in public speaking if one is available. If you take such courses in high school, you will find them easier when you are required to take them again during college or in your program of training to become a legal assistant. Should a college education either before or as a part of your legal assistant training be your wish, these courses should prove advantageous on the verbal portion of the Scholastic Aptitude and Achievement Tests (SAT). This emphasis, however, should not preclude your taking courses in science and mathematics, for these subjects promote the ability to think and reason that will be essential to your success as a legal assistant.

In addition, you should become involved in extracurricular activities as time allows, especially those that develop oral communication skills such as debate, drama, or extemporaneous speaking, and written communication skills such as the yearbook, the creative writing club, or the school newspaper.

Those who seek careers as legal assistants should look at their progress toward that goal as a series of steps. The years spent in high school are surely the stepping-stones for those that will follow. Your record of scholastic and extracurricular achievements in high school may profoundly influence your chances of entering the college or legal assistant training program of your choice. Therefore, try to impress your teachers and others who will influence the course of your future as a person who is a serious and conscientious student. Increase your interest in all of your courses by becoming more involved than is absolutely necessary or required. Take advantage of any opportunities that become available for independent study, or seek them out. The prospective legal assistant will enjoy the reading required by his or her courses and also find enjoyment and pleasure in reading beyond that which is required.

Those who will admit you to the college or program of training of your choice may consider the following factors: your class rank; the general difficulty and nature of the courses you have taken; and opinions of you, your career goals, and your ability to obtain them written by teachers and guidance counselors. The benefits of advanced standing or early graduation may be available to those who take particular care in their preparation for training as legal assistants. Do not be unduly discouraged if your achievement and aptitude test scores are low. Good grades in appropriate courses in high school are often considered as offsetting low test scores on standardized tests.

Other factors are considered when there are more applicants for admission than can be accepted. Admissions office personnel endeavor to consider each applicant as a unique individual and not merely as a composite of tests scores and grades. Extracurricular activities as well as intellectual ability and performance in the classroom are considered. For that reason, you should become active in athletics or student government, for example, seeking to make yourself as well rounded a person as possible.

The number of applicants to any one college or program of training for legal assistants will vary depending on a number of factors. Therefore, first identify a group of colleges or training programs to which you will apply.

In making this initial selection, you can save time, money, and heartache by considering the following factors.

First, determine the type of program in which you are interested. As alluded to previously, three basic types of programs are available. One is a two-year, self-contained program of training at a community, junior, or technical college. Upon completion of the program at such an institution, a degree such as Associate in Arts (A.A.)—Legal Assistant would be awarded to you. Having such a degree, you would be in a position to seek employment as a beginning legal assistant.

The second is a four-year, self-contained program of training at a college or university. Upon completion of such a program, a bachelor's degree in liberal arts (B.A.) or similar degree or a business administration degree (B.S. or B.B.A.) or similar degree is awarded. These degrees would indicate the major field of study as legal assistant. Again, the graduate would be in a position to seek employment as a beginning legal assistant.

The third is a four-year degree program at a college or university with the awarding of a bachelor's degree in some field other than that of legal assistant. The graduate would follow his or her general education with an intensive course of training in subjects to qualify as a practicing legal assistant.

In choosing a program of training, there are three helpful sources of information. One source provides specific information; the other two are sources of general information. For specific information, consult the latest version of the listing of educational institutions offering courses of instruction for legal assistants. This listing, which includes all three of the types of programs discussed above, is issued approximately twice a year by the Standing Committee on Legal Assistants of the American Bar Association, 1155 East 60th Street, Chicago, Illinois 60637. This list attempts to include all institutions offering programs of training for legal assistants, whether or not those programs have received the approval of the American Bar Association, as discussed subsequently.

For general information, the source or sources you consult will depend on the type or types of programs of training you select for initial consideration. You will want to consult the latest edition of the *Community, Junior and Technical College*

Directory, published by the American Association of Community and Junior Colleges, One DuPont Circle N.W., Washington, D.C. 20036; and the *Education Directory, Higher Education* of the United States Department of Health, Education, and Welfare. These and other sources of general information should be available in your local public library, the school library, or the office of the school guidance counselor.

Next determine the admissions policies of the colleges or programs of training in which you are particularly interested. Some educational institutions have an "open admissions" policy, which means that all applicants with a high school diploma or equivalent will be admitted. For legal assistants, some open admissions policies may be qualified by certain communication skills requirements. Open admissions policies or modified open admissions policies are more likely to be found in two-year self-contained programs of training at community, junior, and technical colleges than at four-year degree institutions, whether or not they offer self-contained programs of training. Admission to four-year programs with or without a self-contained major in the field of legal assistant will likely be governed by the same standards as those applied to students who are majoring in other fields. As previously indicated, your rank in your high school class, the nature and quality of the courses you have taken, and the recommendations you can present will be important factors in the admission decision. Programs that require a four-year college degree before admission in general rest their selection process on your meeting this fundamental requirement. Some programs of this type will consider experience and recommendations of present employers in making the admissions decision.

Although most educational institutions or training programs profess an interest in having students from varying geographical backgrounds, most programs seem to favor applicants who are from or near the area. If you hope to become employed as a legal assistant in a particular area of the country, there are at least two distinct advantages of going to school in or near that location. First, programs of instruction may offer opportunities for part-time employment during the summer or while you are attending classes. These employment opportunities, sometimes called "internships," may lead to permanent employment following graduation. Second, while in school, living and working in the community, you may come into contact with graduates who can offer helpful insights into the program of instruction or suggestions as to where to look for full-time employment. Therefore, do not dismiss without careful consideration the thought of obtaining your training close to home or where you wish to become employed.

Consider also the many other factors that should affect your choice. Only you will know what importance or weight to attach to each. They include the location and setting of the educational institution or program of training, cost of tuition, atmosphere, attitude, activities, and numerous other factors.

Do not complete your initial selection process without writing to those programs in which you believe you have an interest. These requests should provide more specific information than you will be able to obtain anywhere else, and it should prove invaluable in making your final selection. On the basis of the information you receive, you may find that your initial interest was based on a wrong impression created by a lack of adequate or current information. Having satisfied yourself with your choices, make formal applications to the institutions or training programs. Consult the materials you have received concerning how soon before your scheduled entrance applications for admission will be accepted. As a final check, you may wish to visit the campus and talk with admissions office personnel, instructors, and students before enrolling.

If you choose to attend college to be trained or before becoming trained as a legal assistant, and even if time and money prevent you from visiting the campus, there are still several things you must do. Some of these requirements may be applicable to noncollegiate programs of training as well. They include the following. Inform the college of your interest. If you do not already have a Social Security number, obtain one from the Social Security Administration before taking the standardized examinations for admission to college and making your application. Fill out and submit the necessary copies of your application together with the application fee. Have mailed from the principal's office a transcript of your high school record to the end of the semester preceding your application, as well as reference letters from the principal, guidance counselor, or teachers who know you personally. In some cases, reports of the scores from the College Entrance Examination Board (CEEB), the SAT, or other achievement tests will be forwarded directly to the colleges you designate at the time you are tested. Be sure to plan to take such examinations sufficiently far in advance to give the college of your choice the opportunity to consider your scores in passing upon your application. Do not wait beyond the fall of your senior year if you expect to be admitted for the fall of the following year. Once notified that your application has been accepted, decide as quickly as possible. When you make your decision, notify the other colleges to which you have made application so that they may consider other applicants. Stand by your mailbox. Materials will begin arriving soon to orient you to your first year on the way to becoming a practicing legal assistant.

CHAPTER III

Education or Training
for Legal Assistants

As indicated in the preceding chapter, the subject of the appropriate educational background for legal assistants is complex and sometimes controversial. Education and/or training as a legal assistant may be acquired in one or both of two contexts: on-the-job training (currently sometimes called in-service training) and formal courses of instruction.

First, let us consider on-the-job or in-service training. Legal assistants, as discussed more fully in Chapter XVI, like lawyers before them, formerly obtained their education or training on the job. The reasons for this were similar. In the early history of the United States, law schools were either nonexistent, geographically remote, or too costly to attend. Persons who wanted to become lawyers received their legal education in the law offices of others, often relatives or friends of the family already engaged in the practice of law. Several early Presidents of the U.S. who were lawyers by profession obtained their legal education in this fashion. These included Presidents James Monroe, John Quincy Adams, Andrew Jackson, Martin Van Buren, James Polk, and Franklin Pierce.

In like manner, the first legal assistants received their education or training on the job. For them, a formal education in the field simply was not available until comparatively recently, despite the fact that there has always been a need for such persons. As discussed further in Chapter XVI, the first legal assistants may have already been employed in law offices or legally related activities as legal secretaries or other clerical personnel. Some were employed by lawyers for the specific purpose of becoming legal assistants through on-the-job training as the only context in which education or training was then available. Most, however, particularly legal secretaries, probably lacked such specific intention. They simply grew into positions as practicing legal assistants. Even today, some lawyers may prefer to train their own legal assistants.

The second context in which education or training for legal assistants may take place is a formal one—through enrollment in and graduation from a legal assistant program administered by an educational institution or training program.

In the late 1960's a number of factors coalesced leading to the creation of formal programs for the education or training of legal assistants. These factors included a growing recognition by present and potential employers of legal assistants that certain persons were already functioning as such, having acquired their skills in service in the absence of formal training programs. Lawyers began to ask themselves why the skills required by legal assistants on the job could not also be taught in the classroom? At about this time, a group of lawyers in Philadelphia formed The Institute for Paralegal Training and created course materials with which to instruct legal assistant generalists and legal assistants in one or more specialties.

Formal training through legal assistant programs is available from educational institutions and training programs that are either public, private, or proprietary. The most outstanding example of the proprietary is The Institute for Paralegal Training in Philadelphia. It accepts only students who hold a bachelor's degree from a four-year college or university or who are sponsored by an existing or prospective employer. So great is its reputation that it has spawned a number of imitators. Unlike public or private educational institutions offering legal assistant programs, proprietary institutions are ultimately in business to make a profit.

At the other extreme is the two-year community, junior, or technical college course for legal assistants. An example of such a program is the one offered by Lakeshore Technical Institute, Cleveland, Wisconsin, beginning in 1975. Currently, 67 credits are required to graduate from the program. These credits include 15 credits of General Education Requirements; 33 credits of (Legal)-Technical Requirements; 13 credits of Related Technical Requirements; and 6 credits of Electives. This total is displayed as follows:

LAKESHORE TECHNICAL INSTITUTE
LEGAL ASSISTANT

COURSE TITLE	CREDITS	
1. General Education Requirements	*15*	
Communication Skills I	3	____
Communication Skills II	3	____
Economics	3	____
Psychology of Human Relations	3	____
American Institutions	3	____
2. Technical Requirements	*33*	
Income Tax Accounting	3	____
Business Law I	3	____
Business Law II	3	____
Introduction to Legal Assistant	3	____
Mechanics of Real Estate	3	____
Administration of Estates	3	____
Domestic Relations	3	____
Creditor/Debtor Relations	3	____
Litigation and Research & Investigative Techniques	3	____
Law Office Management	2	____
Introduction to Corporate Law Practice	3	____
Law Office Ethics	1	____
3. Related Technical Requirements	*13*	
Business Math	3	____
Typing I	3	____
Electives	7	
Choose from		
Accounting I	4	____
Managerial Accounting	4	____
Supervision, Principles of	3	____
Credit Procedures	2	____
Independent Study	1–3	____
Insurance, Principles of	3	____
Power Typewriters	1	____
Record Management	1	____
Introduction to Data Processing	3	____

LAKESHORE TECHNICAL INSTITUTE
LEGAL ASSISTANT
(*continued*)

COURSE TITLE	CREDITS
3. Related Technical Requirements (*continued*)	
Choose from	
Group Interaction	3 _____
Discussion & Meeting Management	2 _____
4. Electives	6

In addition to the two-year or vocational college programs, four-year college programs, and proprietary courses, some law schools offer separate courses of training for legal assistants. The American Bar Association inspects and approves, fully or provisionally, courses that meet its guidelines or meet them within certain limited exceptions that can be corrected. Through the cooperation of the Standing Committee on Legal Assistants of the American Bar Association, a list of institutions offering legal assistant programs is given in Appendix I. No Bar Association approval is indicated in this listing; however, the subject is discussed further in Chapter XXVI.

Legal assistant programs are of three varieties. One type of program trains the person in a specific field of law, procedure, and legal research, such as business organizations (particularly corporations), litigation, probate practice, and real estate law. These specialties are discussed in Chapters V through IX. Another type of program provides general training in the background of English-based American law and procedure and exposes the student to legal research and writing as well as law office management. Persons who take this course are intending to become legal assistant generalists, as discussed in Chapter IV. A third type of program is a combination of the first two. The student, having completed certain courses in English-based American law, legal research, and writing, as well as law office management, may elect additional training in one or more specialties, such as those indicated above.

At the beginning of this chapter, it was indicated that the subject of training for legal assistants is a complex one with many aspects. This complexity and variety of aspects dictate extreme care by the future legal assistant in making the many choices that will be his or hers to make in an effort to reach this professional goal.

Make your choices wisely and well.

CHAPTER IV

Legal Assistant Generalist

Several surveys have been conducted in an effort to determine what legal assistants do. The information provided by such surveys is of particular importance to legal assistant generalists because they may be called upon to do any one or more of a number of tasks—some of which may be familiar and some totally foreign to particular legal assistant specialists. In 1972 and 1973 the American Bar Association conducted one such survey, which showed five tasks legal assistants perform most often. These tasks included searching and checking public records; preparing probate inventories (listings of the assets left by deceased persons to be distributed in accordance with the terms of a will or of state law if the deceased left no will); helping to prepare inheritance and federal and state tax returns; obtaining information from clients either through personal interviews or over the telephone; and indexing documents and preparing digests of facts or law.

A study was conducted in early 1976 by the administration of Lakeshore Technical Institute in implementing the decision to begin a two-year degree program of instruction for legal assistants. This study was called a "Legal Assistant Task Analysis." Sources of information were members of the State Bar of Wisconsin, 71 percent of whom were engaged in the private practice of law, 7 percent of whom were employed by companies or corporations, and the balance of whom (22 percent) were employed by governmental bodies. This survey also sought to determine how trained legal assistants could or would be utilized. Attorneys responding included those in solo practice and in groups of two to five, six to ten, and more than ten. Interestingly, almost half reported that no legal assistants were employed in their offices. This comparatively low figure is undoubtedly attributable in part both to the emerging nature and the lack of definition of the profession. About one-fourth of those responding employed one legal assistant in their offices. The remainder employed as few as two or three to as many as five or more. The purpose of this task analysis was: "To identify tasks usual to the work of the paralegal assistant and to identify tasks potentially a part of legal assistant work in the future." Those to whom the survey was submitted were asked to respond even if they did not currently employ a legal assistant, so that the surveyors might obtain an understanding of "how legal assistants should be used by attorneys." The surveyors predefined tasks performed or capable of being performed by legal assistants and ranked each in two ways: first, "Task Frequency," or how often that task was performed, and second, "Task Importance," which speaks for itself. Results of that survey were published as follows:

Task Number	Task Performed by the Legal Assistant	Task Frequency				Task Importance			
		Never 1	Seldom 2	Often 3	Daily 4	None 1	Low 2	Medium 3	Essential 4
	I. *General Law Office Work*								
	A. *Research*								
	1. Researching law and writing summaries of such research			2.12				3.01	
	2. Preparing briefs of researched cases			2.13				2.77	
	3. Applying research to facts of attorney's case			2.30				2.96	
	B. *Legal Writing*								
	4. Composing office memoranda			2.73				2.88	

Task Number	Task Performed by the Legal Assistant	Task Frequency				Task Importance			
		Never 1	Seldom 2	Often 3	Daily 4	None 1	Low 2	Medium 3	Essential 4
	5. Composing letters to clients		2.77					3.05	
	6. Drafting legal documents		2.55					3.10	
	C. *Interviewing*								
	7. Interviewing clients		2.53					2.90	
	8. Attendance at attorney's interviews of clients		2.37					2.52	
	9. Consulting with attorneys in other firms		2.00					2.34	
	10. Consulting with other staffs		2.59					2.76	
	D. *Law Library*								
	11. General supervision of law library		2.59					2.67	
	12. Choosing titles to be ordered		1.65					2.06	
	13. Updating the law library		2.15					2.49	
	14. Filing pocket parts and library accession duties		2.73					2.86	
II. *Real Estate Problems*									
	A. *Real Estate Sales*								
	15. Clients—initial interviews		2.05					2.54	
	16. Gathering information for offer to purchase		2.49					2.91	
	17. Drafting offer to purchase		2.13					2.73	
	18. Ordering title policy		2.48					2.75	
	19. Obtaining real estate tax record		2.67					2.88	
	20. Obtaining close-out letter for mortgagee		2.38					2.63	
	21. Drafting closing statement		2.31					2.86	
	22. Drafting deeds		2.31					2.90	
	23. Drafting mortgages		2.08					2.71	
	24. Drafting other real estate documents		2.19					2.64	

Task Number	Task Performed by the Legal Assistant	Task Frequency				Task Importance			
		Never 1	Seldom 2	Often 3	Daily 4	None 1	Low 2	Medium 3	Essential 4
	25. Attendance at closing		1.83				2.17		
	26. Conducting closing		1.45				2.19		
B. *Leases*									
	27. Negotiations with tenants or landlords		1.50				2.31		
	28. Drafting leases		1.96				2.53		
	29. Lease renewal negotiations		1.66				2.18		
III. *Estate Planning and Probate*									
A. *Wills*									
	30. Clients—initial interview		1.88				2.60		
	31. Gathering information about assets, insurance, etc.		2.56				2.90		
	32. Drafting wills		1.91				2.56		
	33. Drafting trust documents		1.65				2.40		
	34. Drafting other estate planning documents		1.76				2.51		
B. *Decedents' Estates*									
	35. Clients—initial interview		1.95				2.69		
	36. Gathering information about estate assets and heirs		2.76				3.20		
	37. Drafting documents for filing with courts		2.64				3.06		
	38. Preparing file working papers		2.83				3.08		
	39. Consulting with register in probate		2.51				2.74		
	40. Conducting court hearings		1.45				2.15		
	41. Attendance at court hearings		1.82				2.44		
	42. Docket control		2.62				2.67		
IV. *Commercial Law*									
	43. Clients–initial interview		2.06				2.72		
	44. Gathering information		2.76				3.09		

Task Number	Task Performed by the Legal Assistant	Task Frequency				Task Importance			
		Never	Seldom	Often	Daily	None	Low	Medium	Essential
		1	2	3	4	1	2	3	4
	45. Preparing demand letters		2.60					2.83	
	46. Collections—debtor contacts by telephone		2.50					2.72	
	47. Preparing litigation documents		2.42					2.79	
	48. Docket control		2.70					3.00	
	Small Claims Courts:								
	49. Answering docket call		2.03					2.42	
	50. Pretrial conference	1.79					2.33		
	51. Trial appearance and conducting trial	1.38					2.14		
	Other Courts:								
	52. Pretrial conference		1.54					2.18	
	53. Trial appearance and conducting trial	1.34					2.11		
V. Business Enterprises									
	54. Clients—initial interview	1.78					2.42		
	55. Gathering information		2.59					2.97	
A. Sole Proprietorships									
	56. Licenses, permits, governmental relations		2.03					2.58	
	57. Accounting and tax advice	1.75					2.38		
	58. Collections advice and procedures	1.93					2.39		
B. Partnerships									
	59. Negotiations between prospective partners	1.36					2.17		
	60. Drafting partnership agreement	1.62					2.41		
	61. Legal advice to operating partners	1.39					2.22		
	62. Partnership termination advice and drafting	1.33					2.17		
C. Corporations									
	63. Advice to promoters	1.34					2.16		
	64. Drafting articles of incorporation		2.11					2.65	
	65. Drafting by-laws		2.23					2.74	
	66. Maintenance of corporate minutes		2.35					2.71	

Task Number	Task Performed by the Legal Assistant	Task Frequency				Task Importance			
		Never	Seldom	Often	Daily	None	Low	Medium	Essential
		1	2	3	4	1	2	3	4
	67. Maintenance of other corporate books and records		2.33					2.74	
	68. Dissolution proceedings	1.70					2.38		
	69. Docket control		2.41					2.77	
VI. *Criminal Law*									
	70. Clients—interviewing		2.05					2.65	
	71. Witnesses—interviewing		2.47					3.01	
	72. Investigation of facts		2.62					3.10	
	Traffic violations:								
	73. Negotiations with prosecutors	1.67					2.25		
	74. Court appearances	1.65					2.22		
	Misdemeanors:								
	75. Negotiations with prosecutors	1.59					2.33		
	76. Trial preparation		2.20					2.76	
	77. Trial work	1.56					2.31		
	Felonies:								
	78. Preliminary hearings	1.55					2.31		
	79. Negotiations with prosecutors	1.46					2.26		
	80. Trial preparation		2.17					2.77	
	81. Assisting attorney at trial		2.11					2.71	
	82. Participating in trial	1.52					2.70		
VII. *Domestic Relations*									
	A. *Divorce*								
	83. Clients—interviewing		2.16					2.75	
	84. Other fact gathering		2.70					3.10	
	85. Drafting complaints, motions, affidavits, etc.		2.44					2.86	
	86. Conducting pretrial hearings	1.54					2.16		
	87. Trial preparation		2.09					2.62	
	88. Conducting final hearing	1.37					2.16		
	B. *Juvenile Matters*								
	89. Clients—interviewing	1.83					2.44		
	90. Drafting petitions, etc.	1.93					2.50		
	91. Conducting court hearings	1.41					2.14		
	C. Adoptions								
	92. Clients—interviewing	1.92					2.48		

Task Number	Task Performed by the Legal Assistant	Task Frequency				Task Importance			
		Never 1	Seldom 2	Often 3	Daily 4	None 1	Low 2	Medium 3	Essential 4
	93. Fact and report gathering		2.44					2.86	
	94. Drafting petition, etc.		2.22					2.65	
	95. Conducting hearing		1.42					2.06	
VIII.	*Personal Injury and Other Trial Work*								
	A. *Trial Work*								
	96. Clients—interviewing		1.99					2.71	
	97. Witnesses—interviewing		2.29					2.97	
	Contacts with doctors and other expert witnesses:								
	98. Interviewing		2.04					2.69	
	99. Correspondence		2.45					2.89	
	100. Telephone contacts		2.53					2.95	
	101. Preparing for depositions and other discovery proceedings		2.22					2.78	
	102. Preparation for and drafting of pretrial motions		2.14					2.69	
	103. Preparation for pretrial conference		2.11					2.68	
	104. Preparation for trial		2.27					2.87	
	105. Assisting attorney at trial		2.00					2.52	
	106. Preparation for and drafting of post-trial motions		1.96					2.46	
	107. Entering the judgment		2.17					2.50	
	B. *Appellate Work*								
	108. Drafting notice of appeal and bond		1.94					2.55	
	109. Paging the record for appeal		2.07					2.56	
	110. Summarizing evidence for the appellate brief		1.93					2.63	
	111. Preparing the appellate brief		1.71					2.70	
IX.	*Tax Work*								
	112. Clients—interviewing		2.25					2.84	
	113. Information gathering from account books and records		2.64					3.08	

Task Number	Task Performed by the Legal Assistant	Task Frequency				Task Importance			
		Never 1	Seldom 2	Often 3	Daily 4	None 1	Low 2	Medium 3	Essential 4
114.	Assisting clients in accounting methods and bookkeeping		2.22					2.68	
	Preparation of Returns:								
115.	Individual federal and state		2.56					2.97	
116.	Partnership returns		2.19					2.79	
117.	Corporate returns	1.96						2.70	
118.	Fiduciary returns		2.21					2.83	
119.	Sales tax and others		2.47					2.73	
	Audit procedures:								
120.	Assisting clients	1.88						2.59	
121.	Preparation for audit interviews	1.94						2.58	
122.	Contact with IRS agents, etc.	1.63						2.42	
123.	Conducting audit interviews with agents, etc.	1.50						2.43	

The surveyors' conclusions were as follows: Essential tasks that must be included among the responsibilities of legal assistant generalists included those whose importance ranked 3.00 and above. Eleven tasks fell into this category: I. *General Office Work*, A. *Research*, 1. Researching law and writing summaries of such research, and B. *Legal Writing*, 5. Composing letters to clients. III. *Estate Planning and Probate*, B. *Decedents' Estates*, 36. Gathering information about estate assets and heirs; 37. Drafting documents for filing with courts; and 38. Preparing file working papers. IV. *Commercial Law*, 44. Gathering information, and 48. Docket control. VI. *Criminal Law*, 71. Witnesses—interviewing; and 72. Investigation of facts. VII. *Domestic Relations*, A. *Divorce*, 84. Other fact gathering. IX. *Tax Work*, 113. Information gathering from account books and records. You may want to compare these essential tasks with the five tasks that the 1972–73 American Bar Association survey found legal assistants perform most often. It would also be interesting to learn how legal assistants who have been employed for a year would complete the same survey.

Ninety-six of the tasks were found to be nonessential but nevertheless recommended for inclusion as potential legal assistant responsibilities. Fifteen tasks, those ranking below 2.20, were labeled nonessential tasks. The surveyors recommended that these tasks not be included as ones to be performed by legal assistants. Look again at the results of the survey to see whether or not you agree. These tasks include those that are properly the responsibility of the lawyer, such as conducting lease renewal negotiations, real estate closings, and court hearings.

In the next four chapters, occupational backgrounds for legal assistant specialists in business or corporate law, criminal law, estate work or probate law, litigation, and real estate or property law are discussed. You will note the absence of whole categories of specialization from the responsibilities of the legal assistant generalist. This may be due in part to the small but growing number of legal assistant specialists in these fields of law.

CHAPTER V

Business or Corporate Law Specialist

Each year tens if not hundreds of thousands of new businesses or corporations are formed to accomplish a wide variety of objectives. Each year many of these newly formed businesses or corporations as well as many previously formed fail. The legal assistant who specializes in business or corporate law can be right there in the middle, as well as the beginning and the end, of what is happening.

In any typical on-the-job circumstance, both the lawyer and the legal assistant will be concerned with what type of business organization is most suitable for a particular client. Generally, the choice will be among the sole proprietorship, the partnership, and the corporation. Each has its own advantages and disadvantages, including tax consequences and the availability of benefits to employees such as pension plans.

The business or corporate law specialist will, through a formal program of education or instruction, obtain an understanding of the concept of corporateness. He or she will study both public or publicly held corporations and close or closely held corporations whose shares are held by one or a few shareholders, by examination of state legislation on these subjects.

He or she will learn to prepare and file various documents necessary to form a corporation—the articles of incorporation—and necessary to maintain a corporation, such as annual reports to be filed with the Secretary of State of the state of incorpora-

29

tion. The legal assistant will learn to prepare documents necessary to the internal workings of the corporation such as notices or waivers of notice of regular and/or special meetings of shareholders or directors, and drafts of resolutions to be considered, adopted, amended, or rejected at meetings of shareholders or directors.

The legal assistant may assist in obtaining money to conduct the operations of the business or corporation. He or she may draft agreements to obtain bank loans or money from other lenders. He or she may work with shareholders who wish to make an additional contribution of capital to the corporation and draft documents necessary to effect that result.

Corporations may enter into mergers in which one corporation disappears and the other corporation survives. Corporations may consolidate to form a third corporation. The legal assistant in that case may be involved in the drafting of documents called variously Articles of Merger or Articles of Consolidation and approvals by shareholders or directors necessary to complete these combinations.

The drafting of documents necessary to comply with federal and state securities laws is another possible responsibility for the business or corporate law specialist. The field of securities is now so vast as to be recognized as a distinct specialty in and of itself. There are lawyers who are engaged entirely or almost entirely in securities work, and the same could be true of a legal assistant—a securities law specialist, a specialty within a specialty.

Particularly in the case of close or closely held corporations, the business or corporate law specialist may be involved in the drafting of agreements to restrict the transfer of shares of stock to outsiders, agreements among shareholders to buy one another's shares if certain events take place, such as death, disability, or unwillingness to continue as a shareholder.

Given the subject matter areas in which the business or corporate law specialist may become engaged, you may want to consult again the Legal Assistant Task Analysis presented in

Chapter IV to note the frequency and importance of tasks that may be performed by this specialist. If you are particularly interested in this specialty, rerank the tasks listed in order of frequency and importance from highest to lowest.

The business or corporate law specialist may be involved from time to time with direct client contact. These contacts could occur under any circumstance but are especially likely to take place at the time of the initial client interview. The business or corporate law specialist would do well to learn early the special relationship that must be established and preserved between the lawyer-employer and the client. Remember that the services performed by the business lawyer are not clearly and immediately visible to the client. Therefore, both the lawyer and, to the extent he or she is involved, the legal assistant must create and maintain a favorable personal and professional impression. Little things can and do mean a lot—promptness and other attributes of common courtesy as well as the proper attitude and demeanor are all vitally important.

Perhaps the best advice that can be given to the business or corporate law specialist is to be and remain yourself. Remember that you are in a particularly advantageous position. You may in fact have more contact with clients at critical times than your employer. During the course of these contacts, be sensitive to matters that may adversely affect the relationship between the lawyer and the client. The client may be reluctant to discuss these directly with the lawyer. You may have the unique opportunity, as discretely as possible, to set matters right again.

CHAPTER VI

Criminal Law Specialist

Exposure to criminal law through television, movies, newspapers, magazines, or even in their personal lives may lead many to this career field with the idea, expressed or unexpressed, that they would become criminal law specialists. Unfortunately, the criminal law specialist may not experience the degree of excitement that appears to have been promised. Nevertheless, challenging careers are available in this field, whether you are employed by an arm of the state or a person or group charged with criminal conduct.

In preparation for a career as a criminal law specialist, the legal assistant may be instructed in formal programs as to basic distinctions between law among private parties, or civil law, and criminal law, the rights of society vis-à-vis the individual members of society. He or she is likely to be instructed as to who participates in the criminal justice system and the roles they play.

The criminal law specialist will learn both the procedure—how and where, and the substance—what human conduct is prohibited. He or she will also be taught the importance of defenses to conduct alleged to be criminal, including defenses based upon the Bill of Rights or other federal or state constitutional provisions.

Criminal law specialists will learn techniques for investigating both the law and the facts as background for trials. They will also learn to prepare for the trial of a criminal matter, including the preparation of motions in the various stages before trial and how they can assist their lawyer employers during the course of the trial, including keeping track of documents and evidence and keeping files continually updated.

Criminal law specialists will also learn how they can assist after trial. All of this knowledge, acquired both formally and on the job, will be highly useful in their daily activities. Again you may want to examine the appropriate section of Chapter IV to determine which activities of the criminal law specialist are ranked as occurring most frequently and being of most importance. You will find "Investigation of facts" ranked highest both as to frequency and importance.

CHAPTER VII

Estate Work or Probate Law Specialist

In order for the estate work or probate law specialist to find employment, someone must die. Since we will all die sooner or later, the estate work or probate law specialist is perhaps more assured than most other legal assistants of continued employment. Death, like life, also means taxes. All kinds of taxes—federal estate taxes, gift taxes, and usually state inheritance taxes as well. Combining two certainties like death and taxes further assures employment for the estate work or probate law specialist.

An estate is what a person leaves behind at the time of his death. A person dies either testate (leaving a will) or intestate (not leaving a will). Probate is the process of accumulating and distributing that property left at death to those who are legally entitled to have it either under the terms of the will or by virtue of the laws of intestate succession.

Estate work or probate law specialists are deeply involved in this process. Among their responsibilities they may: (1) prepare probate petitions; (2) prepare inventories of assets; (3) prepare tax returns; (4) transfer and register securities; (5) attend settlements of real estate matters; (6) perform accounting functions such as maintaining checkbooks, journals, and ledgers as well as preparing accountings; (7) distribute assets of the estate to those entitled to take; and (8) draft wills. If you consult the appropriate section of Chapter IV, you will find that gathering information, whether a person has died testate or intestate, is ranked as the activity of the highest frequency and importance for the estate work or probate law specialist.

CHAPTER VIII

Litigation Specialist

2067300

Life for the litigation specialist is a whole new world of plaintiffs (people who sue) and defendants (people who have been sued) and civil suits (not additions to your wardrobe but litigation between private parties).

Typically, the litigation specialist will, through a formal program of education or training, learn to do the following: (1) draft pleadings—legal documents in law suits stating the positions of the various parties—for example, complaints (petitions) for plaintiffs, answers (replies) for defendants, and motions for either side; (2) draft interrogatories—questions by one party to another, answers to interrogatories, and requests for production of documents, for example, a policy or policies of insurance in a personal injury case; (3) digest depositions—formal interviews with potential witnesses; (4) index and summarize documents; (5) obtain records and reports; (6) prepare evaluations of cases for purposes of making decisions to settle or to proceed to trial of a case; (7) prepare stipulations—written agreements between parties or their attorney—and orders for dismissal of cases that are pending, releases, and settlement agreements; (8) draft notices, affidavits (sworn statements), and motions and petitions (requests for specific relief); (9) verify and Shepardize (determine the subsequent history) of cases, statutes, rules and regulations; and (10) maintain dockets (lists of actions to be taken at specified times) and files.

During the course of education or training, litigation specialists will learn the distinction between civil and criminal litigation, emphasizing civil litigation; be exposed to procedures governing the conduct of law suits; and learn the importance of legal precedent established by cases previously decided involving similar facts and what types of relief—sometimes called remedies—a court may provide.

Litigation specialists will learn about the system of dual courts in the U.S.—both state and federal—and the specific rules of procedure that apply to court proceedings. Students should be provided with a brief overview of the various areas of substantive law that they may encounter. Those specific subject matters mentioned and explained may include contracts, torts (private wrongs) including intentional and negligent or careless wrongdoing, as well as the concept of strict liability in the case of products defective in manufacture that are proven to have caused injury; and business or corporate law, including securities law.

Litigation specialists, having received their formal education or training, will be prepared to assist the lawyer in a number of ways. Based on the information provided in Chapter IV, the most frequent tasks that will be performed are telephone contacts in preparation for trial. This reflects the statistical probability that any given case will be settled at some point in the course of preparation for trial and before trial begins. In like fashion, litigation specialists are more likely to be involved in the trial of a case than in its appeal. Again this reflects the statistical probability that most cases that proceed to judgment will not be appealed for any one of a number of reasons, including the cost or the absence of plausible grounds for appeal.

This is not to deny the importance of appellate work, as indicated by the ratings listed in Chapter IV. In fact, as a litigation specialist, you may wish to make your career in appellate work, a subspecialty of the litigation specialist.

CHAPTER IX

Real Estate or Real Property Law Specialist

Many success books written yesterday and today subscribe to the theory that there are personal fortunes to be made by those who knowledgeably invest in real estate or real property. Be that as it may, the legal assistant who is a real property or real estate law specialist can make a comfortable living in an interesting field.

Based on information supplied in Chapter IV, real estate or real property law specialists are involved in leases and sales of real property, although generally more frequently in sales than in leases. This distinction is perhaps attributable to the likelihood that the employer of the legal assistant is more frequently involved with sales of property than with leases. There is no indication that the activities of the real estate or real property law specialist are in any way restricted.

With respect to leases, this specialist may be drafting leases, participating in lease renewal negotiations, or negotiating with tenants or landowners. The legal assistant aspects of real estate sales include the following: (1) initial client interviews, gathering information for and drafting offers to purchase; (2) preparations for closing, including obtaining the real estate tax record, ordering the title policy, and, when required, obtaining a close-out letter for a mortgagee—one who has lent money on the property; (3) preparation or drafting of documents, including deeds, mortgages, other real estate documents, and the closing statement; and (4) attendance at or conducting the closing.

The real estate or real property law specialist is involved with varying degrees of frequency every step of the way. Some of these steps, particularly the conducting of the closing, approach or may constitute the practice of law. To the extent that this is true, the involvement of the legal assistant is—by definition— reduced.

CHAPTER X

Satisfactions of a Legal Assistant Career

Both personal and professional satisfactions will be found by those who enter upon careers as legal assistants. In that respect, such a career offers the most you could wish from any career. Without seeking to oversell it, work as a legal assistant, while not the thrill-a-minute that very few careers are, is clearly and constantly challenging to those who are willing to make it so. In addition, work as a legal assistant is important and meaningful. If you will participate and not merely observe, professional advancement can be yours. By benefiting yourself, you will also help others—the rest of the members of the legal services team as well as the clients who are served and society at large. In doing so, give of your best and cooperate with others, resting firm in the belief that they will do likewise.

Unlike some careers, work as a legal assistant provides those in the field with many chances to see how people have been helped directly and immediately by the work they have done or of which they have been an integral and important part. Examples are many—for domestic relations and an adoption, they have the knowledge that a couple who perhaps could not otherwise have been parents are now a proud mamma and papa and a baby has a loving home. For criminal law, they know that a person falsely accused has been vindicated, or that a person charged with murder has been tried, found guilty, and sentenced and will no longer be a threat to society.

Accompanying life for all of us are opportunities as well as problems. Developing the ability to see as an opportunity what might seem to be a problem is the goal of the Optimists, members of a major international service club. Like the Optimists, as you deal with legal matters, you will find both challenge and satisfaction in being able to enhance others' opportunities and mitigate their problems. You must like people, or you wouldn't have consulted this book. Know then that helping people is a significant job satisfaction of a legal assistant career.

Opportunities for both specific and general self-improvement should flow from continuing experience as a practicing legal assistant. These opportunities, too, are significant personal and job satisfactions. Perhaps you yourself, your family, or friends have experienced or will experience a legal problem. As you gain experience as a practicing legal assistant, you will acquire a better understanding of approaches to solving legal problems. In the course of your employment, you will have helped your employer many times with matters in which you have no personal interest. He or she may be willing to help you, with your assistance again, toward a resolution of any such troubling personal circumstances that could not otherwise be economically resolved.

As you pursue your legal assistant career, you will discover that nearly all you experience or would hope to experience has or would have a legal consequence, some pleasant and some less so. As indicated previously, should you first become employed as a legal assistant by a general practitioner, your employer's practice may range from the law of arbitration to the law of zoning. Moreover, you will find, as you progress through your career, that your first employment may lead to discovery of new interests and specialties.

Give yourself the opportunity to pursue your career as a legal assistant as your changing interests and realizations may indicate. Do not confine yourself to inflexible attitudes about the type of legal assistant employment you should continue or seek, its location, or setting. Do not restrict yourself to being a generalist for the remainder of your career should you subsequently become interested in a particular specialty. But do consider that it will probably be far easier to become a specialist after practicing as a generalist than vice versa. Unless you are very certain of your specialty at the outset, therefore, you will first seek a broad range of experience before deciding on the specialty that is right for you.

The opportunity to advance yourself on the same job or by changing employment, without additional formal education, is there to be found. Endeavor to keep up by continuing your education on an informal basis whenever and wherever you are able to do so. As your range and depth of experience increase, more exciting and better-paying job opportunities should become available to you. This should be true even for those who as a matter of choice do not seek careers as specialists in urban settings. More specific information on positions for legal assistants and applicable salaries is given in Chapter XV.

It is very unlikely that one who pursues a legal assistant career will become technologically obsolete. The very nature of the fields of law and of legal assistant dictates that. Despite the competition for positions that has been mentioned earlier, other factors—not the least of which is the economics of the delivery of legal services—indicate that there will be a steady and gradually increasing demand for people with appropriate background and training to serve as legal assistants. Because of the emerging nature of the field, those who enter it now or within the next several years should, if they pursue their careers intelligently, have an inherent advantage over Johnny-come-latelies.

All work and no play makes anyone a dull person. In pursuing a career as a legal assistant, you will find there are a number of social aspects to the field. Your work will require your close cooperation with other members of the team. These social contacts may be as stimulating and rewarding as the work itself. Ideas, assistance, and mutual help can be shared with others in the field who work in your office or elsewhere. In addition to the development of working relationships, close personal relationships may develop on the job or elsewhere. Marriage to someone with whom you can share like career goals is a distinct possibility.

The following chapter considers employment opportunities for legal assistants that may not be as obvious as others. Education or training for legal assistant careers yields many opportunities. It can and should be a stimulating career for you; at times, perhaps, a bit overly stimulating. Approached properly, a legal assistant career will keep you interested and involved as can few other careers.

Even though legal services are delivered as the consequence of team action, many satisfying results will be achieved that are clearly traceable to your personal efforts. This is the essence of personal and job satisfactions provided by a legal assistant career. Although these satisfactions may be enhanced by location or setting, kind of employer, and choice of work as well as reduced by outside factors such as the needs or wishes of your spouse or family or the job itself, they are not to be denied whatever your situation. As your working life continues, it should be possible to manage your career and its requirements, interaction on the job, and social contacts toward the particular circumstances that are best for you.

CHAPTER XI

Less Obvious Job Opportunities

In Chapter IV the legal assistant generalist was discussed, and a number of responsibilities that such a person might perform were described. In Chapters V through IX specific legal assistant specialties were discussed. In addition, two other specialties, domestic relations or family law specialist and credit and collection or commercial law specialist are mentioned in Chapter XXI in discussing group legal services. Chapter XIX, discussing the kinds of legal assistant work, indicates specific jobs for which legal assistants might be employed in federal, state, or local government with the executive, legislative, or judicial branches or administrative or regulatory agencies. This chapter, as its title indicates, will be devoted to less obvious job opportunities. These are jobs you would want or perhaps might prefer over the traditional ones—if only you had thought of them.

Three suggestions are offered for your consideration. They are based on the headlines in today's newspapers. If tomorrow's news is different from today's, as it undoubtedly will be, you can be certain that, with a little intelligent probing, it will reflect jobs to be done by legal assistants.

The first suggestion is consumer law specialist. "Consumerism" is a word attributed by some solely to Ralph Nader. Nader and his Raiders tend to concentrate on consumer issues of nationwide import for which the law may offer solutions, including unsafe automobiles and other hazards to the public health, safety, or welfare. Twenty years ago, when you were perhaps yet unborn, there were no admonitions on consumer goods: "WARNING: This product may be hazardous to your health."

While all of this is of great moment, consumer law specialists, on a somewhat lesser scale, have the opportunity to make singular and significant contributions to clients and to society. As the job title indicates, they do not do the work of the business or corporate law specialist, for example. However, they will be doing almost all the other things that a legal assistant generalist would do. Problems with which they could become involved might include those between landlord and tenant from the tenant's viewpoint, commercial law from the debtor's side, and litigation—either plaintiff or defendant. It is the consumer law specialist who will be more likely to be involved in work that will change the world—or at least a little piece of it—for the better. If you are a crusader, you may well wish to consider becoming a consumer law specialist.

A second suggestion is energy law specialist. Although energy, both conservation and new sources of energy, are today's headlines, the subject of energy in some aspect is likely to be in the headlines for years to come. You could find interesting work as an energy law specialist and perhaps contribute to solving—or at least obtaining a better understanding of—one of the greatest problems mankind has ever faced.

A third suggestion is international law specialist. This would probably be a subspecialty practiced by a business or corporate law specialist. Excitement is heightened by the addition of transactions in the context of international law and perhaps a foreign language.

These three suggestions are merely illustrative of what may have been to you less than obvious job opportunities. You may want to dig a little deeper for yourself. Find a topic that interests you and do some further research. Always keep in mind whether your interests will correspond with where the jobs will be and the geographical area in which you wish to locate. As you narrow your interests, read this chapter again in conjunction with Chapter XIII on the subject of geography.

CHAPTER XII

Opportunities for Advancement

Elsewhere in this book, particular opportunities for legal assistants are discussed. These discussions include types of responsibilities for legal assistants in Chapters IV through IX and kinds of employers in Chapter XIX. This chapter will be devoted to the subject of opportunities for advancement by legal assistants. The concept of advancement, however, will be construed broadly to include opportunities for change as well as upward mobility.

Six subcategories of opportunities for advancement or change will be discussed: (1) from the field of legal assistant to a perhaps more prestigious career in the field of law; (2) from legal assistant generalist to one or another of the specialties; (3) from one of the specialties to legal assistant generalist; (4) from one specialty to another specialty; (5) from one of the specialties to a subspecialty; and (6) within the category of legal assistant generalist or one of the legal assistant specialties.

In the first instance, a change from a legal assistant to a probably more prestigious career in the field of law would be considered by most as a professional advancement. The field of legal assistant is a recognized job category in and of itself, however, and legal assistants do not move, as a matter of course, for example, to lawyer to judge. Becoming a lawyer requires at least six and usually seven years of education beyond high school, including a bachelor's degree in some field of study. Admission to the bar, usually by successfully completing a written examination, is also required before a person is entitled to practice law. To become a judge, you must almost always first be a lawyer and subsequently be either appointed or elected. In contrast, the legal assistant may become educated or trained in the field in as short a time as two years or even less. Lawyers and judges, therefore, are legitimately concerned about legal assistants becoming involved in the unauthorized practice of law.

On the other hand, it is possible for a legal assistant generalist to become a specialist in one or more of the legal assistant specialties. Despite the description "legal assistant generalist," such a person will become involved in certain activities or tasks more than others. The legal assistant generalist may thus evolve. Such an evolution may be an advancement or merely a change, depending on the circumstances. It may occur by virtue of personal preference or be dictated by employment circumstances.

In contrast, it is much less probable that the legal assistant specialist will become a legal assistant generalist or switch from one distinct specialty to another. The specialist has acquired valuable abilities and skills; it would require unusual circumstances to indicate or dictate such changes. The one exception may be the case of the consumer law specialist discussed in Chapter XI. He or she, having responsibilities in the nature of a legal assistant generalist, might quite readily assume that role under the proper circumstances.

The legal assistant specialist might wish to or be asked to develop a subspecialty. One example seems appropriate. The business or corporate law specialist might well become a subspecialist in any of a number of areas—a credit and collection or commercial law specialist; an international (business) law specialist, a securities law specialist, or a tax law specialist.

Perhaps the greatest hope for advancement is to persevere in your first or present position. Both legal assistant generalists and those engaged in particular specialties should be able to advance in their present positions as they become increasingly valuable to their employers by improving old abilities and skills and acquiring new ones.

Should personal circumstances or a lack of job satisfaction dictate a different job, review your present circumstances and the contents of this chapter before you determine to make a change. Whatever you decide to do, as always, look before you leap!

CHAPTER XIII

Geographical Location

As of August, 1977, according to the compilation of the Standing Committee on Legal Assistants of the American Bar Association, more than two hundred programs were in existence for the education or training of legal assistants. Thirty-nine of the continental United States, Alaska, Hawaii, and the District of Columbia listed one or more such educational institutions or training programs. States not offering such courses of instruction were Arkansas, Idaho, Maine, Montana, New Hampshire, North Dakota, Rhode Island, South Dakota, and Wyoming. By February, 1978, a legal assistant program was being offered in New Hampshire. The number and dispersion of legal assistant programs is likely to grow at least arithmetically if not geometrically over the next decade. This increasing number and dispersion of formal courses of instruction will provide the legal assistant with a greater number of choices of community and geographical location in which to obtain education or training.

Another factor bearing on the eventual geographical location in which the legal assistant may become employed is the growing number of people in the U.S. who are or will in the foreseeable future be licensed to practice law. The 1970 decennial census put the total population of the U.S. at 204,765,770. With approximately 400,000 lawyers practicing or eligible to practice law in the U.S., this means that there is one lawyer for every five to six hundred members of the general population. Theoretically, therefore, the opportunity for employment as a legal assistant exists almost everywhere throughout the country. Practically speaking, however, there are several restrictions, some of which are rather severe. This chapter, then, will be devoted to a discussion of the factors that will or should affect a planned choice of location in which to obtain your training and your first job as a legal assistant. In choosing location or community, planning is the most important factor over which you will have a degree of control. In this regard, you can either plan or fail to plan. Planning may well help you to avoid a mistake or mistakes—wasted time, unnecessary effort, and expense—that you might otherwise make.

The theory of the wide availability of jobs for competent legal assistants first breaks down when you realize that education or training in a particular community or geographical location does not assure you of obtaining employment there or even nearby. Depending on your present location, you may have to consider carefully the wisdom of moving to another location in order to obtain your training. The following factors are yours to consider.

First, as the states become increasingly homogeneous, the laws of the several states (in part because of the passage of so-called uniform legislation) become less and less different. Yet today there exist and tomorrow there will still exist significant differences in the laws and approaches to legal matters among the states. You will be most likely to learn these important differences by obtaining your training as a legal assistant in the state or jurisdiction in which you wish to find employment. Your choice of the place to study, then, should ultimately be strongly influenced by the location in which you wish to find employment. For example, prospective law students are advised to enroll in law schools or colleges of law in the states in which they wish to practice. The vast majority of students graduating from law school are required to pass a written examination, usually covering both their knowledge of basic legal subjects and their knowledge of their professional responsibilities. There is a limited exception called "diploma privilege" for students who have graduated from a college or school of law in the jurisdiction in which they are admitted to practice and have taken certain prescribed courses.

Unlike lawyers and others, legal assistants need not yet be licensed to practice. But if and when state legislatures should declare that legal assistants must be licensed, those who have obtained their education and training in the jurisdiction of their employment will have an advantage in obtaining that license.

Second, examine the supply of and demand for legal assistants in the geographical location and preferably the community in which you wish to work. If that location is not your present one, spend the time and money necessary to visit with the administrators and educators as well as placement personnel of programs for education of legal assistants in the areas of your interest. During your visit, in addition to talking with placement personnel, specifically discuss job opportunities with students and recent graduates. Temper your expectations of obtaining employment if the geographical area or community has an educational institution offering a legal assistant program. This is particularly true in the smaller community. A certain percentage of graduates will wish to locate there, and as a consequence the job market may become quickly saturated. For example, examine the listing of educational institutions offering legal assistant programs. Do not choose to enroll in the program at Iowa Lakes Community College, Estherville, Iowa (population, 1970 Census, 7,998), expecting later to find employment there. The same can be said of the program at Midway College, Midway, Kentucky (population, 1970 Census, 1,246).

Also be aware of a related problem in connection with the supply of and demand for graduates of legal assistant programs. Again refer to the listing of educational institutions offering legal assistant programs. Note, for example, the existence of two programs by two different institutions in Littleton, Colorado, which for some is a highly desirable place in which to live and go to school. For that reason, the supply of legal assistants who wish to locate in Littleton, Colorado (Population, 1970 Census,

23,643) is likely to exceed the demand. For another example, the listing includes five programs in the Phoenix, Arizona, area, which the local Chamber of Commerce calls the Valley of the Sun. This area boasts rapid growth over the past three decades, but the supply of legal assistants who are graduating from programs offered there may at some point outpace the demand. Again, the special attention paid to the question of placement before entering any particular program should be well worth the effort expended.

Third, give some thought to the field of law in which you would like to become employed. Should you desire to assist a lawyer specializing in domestic relations matters, for example, The Institute for Paralegal Training in Philadelphia does not offer such a specialty. Other legal assistant programs may offer one or more courses in this specialty or the opportunity for independent study to secure sufficient credits to constitute a specialty or emphasis. Moreover, the specialty of your choice and the selection of geographical area or community in which to obtain your education and to seek employment are not entirely separate and independent considerations. For example, look for a legal assistant program offering a specialization in labor law in an industrialized locale, not in a small community or rural area.

CHAPTER XIV

Can You Set Up Your Own Business in the Field of Legal Assistant?

This book has continually stressed the legal services team and the role of the legal assistant as a crucial member of that team. The days of a lawyer working with only a legal secretary to help him or her may well be numbered, for a group of converging reasons. These reasons include economic and physical limitations and the growing complexity of particular fields of law that make specialization in group practice the probable wave of the future. Increasingly today and for the foreseeable future, lawyers, like other professionals, will carry on their activities in organizations staffed by an assemblage of salaried employees. If present trends continue, legal assistants should occupy an increasingly large percentage of this group. Initially, then, you should know that certain practical considerations make it unlikely that you will be able to or want to set up your own business in the field of legal assistant.

In addition, the opportunities for legal assistants to work successfully on a full-time self-employed basis, maximizing their independence, are further restricted by the ethical considerations discussed in Chapter I. It is fundamental to the activities of the legal assistant that he or she can function only under the supervision of the lawyer-employer. Because the lawyer-employer directs and supervises the work of the legal assistant and obtains the benefits of the work product, the lawyer is held ultimately responsible should the legal assistant err. This ethical consideration, then, more than any other reason, prevents the legal assistant from setting up in business. Nevertheless, within and operating as a member of a legal services team, it is still possible for the legal assistant to exercise a considerable amount of discretion, independence, and autonomy. The balance of this chapter, therefore, will discuss how the legal assistant operates freely as a member of the legal services team.

First, the competence of the legal assistant leads to independence and freedom of action on any particular job. The legal assistant should try to be as good at what he or she does as possible. Tasks accomplished promptly and correctly will increase the stature of the legal assistant among other members of the legal services team, particularly the lawyer-employer, increasing the lawyer's dependence on the services of the legal assistant. Being able to function in this manner, the legal assistant works with a level of ability and skill that even the lawyer-employer perhaps could not attain. Moreover, he or she is the only member of the legal services team who is able to perform effectively the tasks of a legal assistant. The legal assistant utilizes abilities and skills that other members of the team do not possess.

Second, as your competence increases, you will be able to exercise more and more discretion not only as to the mechanics or methods of accomplishing particular results, but also as to the independence and freedom of action to know those mountains that you can climb alone and those that you cannot scale without assistance from other members of the team. To a large extent, this independence and freedom of action belie the notion mentioned in Chapter I that the legal assistant can be of help to her employer and the legal services team only in matters of a routine nature. Matters that in the office where you are employed were never before considered routine can, in your capable and responsible hands, become so. Your independence and freedom of action to a large degree are what you have made them.

Third, the competence of the legal assistant provides the independence and freedom of action to change jobs if and when it should become necessary to do so. As discussed subsequently in Chapter XVII, there may come a time when your initial preference to make continued progress in your present employment is or seems to be no longer possible. The competence you have acquired as a legal assistant should give you a feeling of independence and freedom of action to go out and seek an alternative position.

CHAPTER XV

The Financial Rewards
of a Legal Assistant Career

Any discussion of compensation for legal assistants or other members of the legal services team is certain to be a bit dated by the time you read this book. The wage or salary or yearly income statistics cited here will be affected by the then present supply and demand for legal assistants and the contributions they can make, as well as by what seem to be inevitable increases in the cost of living and action by government or reaction to then current economic conditions.

Taking all of these factors into consideration, incomes of legal assistants will probably rise for the foreseeable future, but perhaps not as fast as the cost of living. Moreover, it is possible that growing attempts to unionize white-collar workers will ultimately strongly affect the incomes of those who work as legal assistants. In this regard, feelings of pinched pocketbooks may one day overcome or be found no longer inconsistent with attitudes of professionalism. Legal assistants may unionize and use the tactics of unions such as strikes and picketing to obtain the increases in pay they may believe they can obtain in no other way.

The income outlook for legal assistants for the near-term future is decidedly cloudy, the result of both the emerging nature and the lack of definition of the occupation and the competition among graduates to obtain worthwhile positions in the field.

Official salary summaries are scarce, and those that are available may be of doubtful validity. To the extent possible, this chapter will provide the latest information available during the course of the preparation of this book.

Although the incomes of doctors and other members of the health team who provide medical care are currently soaring, the same cannot be said in general of compensation for lawyers. For example, it has been estimated that the average income of lawyers is $26,500. Doctors are said to average more than twice that amount each year.[1]

The word "average" as used in this context is capable of more than one interpretation. Presumably it indicates the median annual income: half of the lawyers in the U.S. make more than $26,500 a year and half earn less. Of those who earn less than the median, some may be satisfied because they lack higher expectations. The remainder who earn less than the median, if not satisfied, have been unable, for whatever reasons, to do better.

In any event, if this interpretation is correct, the annual income levels that can be expected by legal assistants employed by lawyers falling in the bottom half of the income scale will be thereby somewhat restricted. This will be true despite your belief that your training and abilities entitle you to a greater income and a higher standard of living.

The financial picture, then, may not be as promising as you may have anticipated. As you read further, however, remember that there are factors other than direct pay that should affect your employment decision-making. These fringe benefits, including the possibility of paid vacations, medical and dental care, hospitalization, term life insurance plans, and pension plans, may play an important part in your decision. Some of these benefits are highly desirable, and they would otherwise come out of your pocket or purse. If you are thinking about making a change in your employment, an increase in direct pay and fringe benefits may be offset by personal and job satisfactions in your present position.

[1] *Time,* April 10, 1978, p. 56.

A pleasant working relationship in which a high value is placed on you and your work could easily be replaced in a new position with an unhappy job situation.

CURRENT SALARIES BASED ON AVAILABLE INFORMATION

Personal Observations

As part-time coordinator of the Legal Assistant Course Program at Lakeshore Technical Institute, Cleveland, Wisconsin, with the responsibility, among others, to assist the Placement Director in finding jobs for graduates, I have gathered some personal observations on the subject of wages, salaries, and incomes that may reasonably be expected by recent graduates. By way of background, as discussed elsewhere in this book, Lakeshore Technical Institute offers a two-year self-contained program of education in the field of legal assistant. Upon completion of the program, graduates receive the degree of Associate in Arts with a major in Legal Assistant. Graduates seeking their first employment in the immediate geographic area of the school can expect to receive initial compensation from something more than the minimum hourly wage (as of this writing, $2.65 per hour), or not much more than $5,500 per year to as much as $8,000 per year. The higher salaries are available to those with additional education or specific abilities also useful in a law office, particularly legal secretarial skills. Those willing or able to settle in a larger city such as Milwaukee or who are otherwise exceptional may expect initial annual compensation as high as $10,000 or more. Although no statistics are currently available concerning the expectable range of compensation, the high end of the range probably approaches twice the beginning compensation, adjusted for increases in the cost of living. Another measure of the high end of the compensation range might be the starting salary that a recent law school graduate accepting employment with that office might anticipate.

*Specific Information from Educational Institutions or
Training Programs*

The Institute for Paralegal Training in Philadelphia has indicated in recruiting applicants for its programs of training that, based on past history, its graduates can expect an average starting salary in major cities of $$9,400 per year. In New York the average is said to be $10,700.[2] Specific salaries will be affected by precise location and course of training.

Chronicle Guidance Publications, Inc., Moravia, New York 13118, publishes "Occupational Briefs" discussing differing aspects of various careers. The document for legal assistants offers the following information concerning expectable starting salaries:[3]

They can expect a starting salary between $8,000 and $10,500. In 1977 the minimum starting salary of legal assistants in New York City was about $9,000. Starting salaries in the Washington, D.C., metropolitan district ranged from $8,000 to $12,000.

In 1976 paralegals in the Office of the Solicitor earned from $10,520 to $15,481 a year. Most legal assistants have a GS-7 rating. Ratings range from GS-5 to GS-13.

If you are interested in employment with the federal government, you should investigate the GS ratings for legal assistants employed by the particular agency, branch, or office of your interest as well as the salary ranges that those GS ratings represent. If you are interested in employment in state government, data similar to that of the federal government concerning positions and salary ranges may be public information that you can obtain before making your employment decision.

In another chapter, in choosing your program of instruction, you were encouraged to write to the schools of your choice for

[2] *Lawyer's Assistant Catalog* (1978), The Institute for Paralegal Training, Philadelphia, p. 3.
[3] 3d ed. D.O.T. 119,288, printed November, 1977, p. 1.

information. When you write, you should inquire about salary expectations as well as placement facilities and the historical record of placement for graduates.

Relevant Factors

The absolute figures set forth previously from whatever sources, whether starting salaries or salary ranges, offer little guidance for decision-making. More relevant, perhaps, is a discussion of two of the factors that tend to affect levels of compensation, starting salaries, and salary ranges. These two factors are: (1) location of the job, geography and community; and (2) generalization versus specialization.

Location of the Job, Geography and Community

For our purposes, location of the job as to geography and community is synonymous with cost of living. Generally, salaries will be higher on the East Coast (New York State and New York City) or the West Coast (California and Los Angeles or San Francisco) than they will be in the Midwest, the South, or the Southwest. The cost of living is higher in the former areas than in the latter. By the same token, salaries will be higher in urban areas than in smaller communities or rural areas.

On the other hand, the urban lawyer is usually a member of a firm consisting of many lawyers. Just as economics dictate that the general practitioner cannot afford to specialize, the urban practitioner usually cannot afford not to specialize. Partners and associates of large city firms usually need a legal assistant with particular training or skills in only one field of law.

As a consequence of these distinctions, the legal assistant employed by a general practitioner may command a smaller starting salary than the legal assistant with a specialization. Again, this may be a result of the location of the practice rather than status as a generalist or specialist. The generalist may have an advantage over the specialist, at least initially, in changing employment. Whereas the initial salary of the generalist may be lower, the salary range of the generalist may be broader than that of the specialist. In addition, the skills of the specialist may, without continuing education, become obsolete. The skills of the generalist are likely to increase as he or she conquers one new challenge after another on the job.

In addition, among particular specialties, if incomes enjoyed by lawyers are any indication, salaries to be received by legal assistants are likely to be greater in certain areas of specialization than in others. For example, lawyers who specialize in corporation law or in a probate practice are likely, on average, to earn more per year than their counterparts in the criminal law field.

In summary, as your experience increases and your abilities and skills are maintained and enhanced, your level of income increases in accordance with your greater value to your employer.

CHAPTER XVI

Kinds of People in Legal Assistant Careers

As stated in Chapter I, women predominate over men in the legal assistant field. However, as is discussed in Chapter XXIV, there are opportunities in the field for men, women, the disadvantaged, members of minority groups, and others.

The predominance of women as legal assistants is largely because women had roles in law offices or legally related activities as legal secretaries or other clerical personnel long before the legal assistant concept received its current recognition. It is estimated that women are becoming employed as legal assistants at an increasingly earlier age. Today, based on personal observation and without statistical data to support it, the median age of legal assistants is estimated at twenty-five years or less. This is a substantial change in the kinds of people, especially women, in legal assistant work within only the past ten years.

In the late 1960's before the advent of formal programs of education and training, the typical legal assistant, while still a woman, was of a median age as much as twenty years older than currently. One kind of legal assistant probably had no formal education or training in the work. She acquired her knowledge from a lifetime on the job, probably with the same employer and probably as a legal secretary. By observation, doing, or instruction, such people acquired abilities and skills beyond the legal secretarial or clerical skills for which they were first employed.

Both lawyers and clerical personnel came to look to them for answers to practical questions.

A second kind of legal assistant of the late 1960's and early 1970's was a woman, perhaps a housewife with children in school or grown, who was hired by a law office or legally related activity to assist in accomplishing a particular major objective. An example might be the development of facts to prosecute or defend complex litigation. Such person would search and organize files and develop and verify facts. Complex litigation may continue for three to five years or longer. Once the litigation was completed, the need for that employee would seem to be at an end. However, many such people, having long since convinced their lawyer-employers of their indispensability, stayed on and developed into functioning legal assistants.

The theory of the late 1970's is that the modern legal assistant is more in the nature of the latter example than the former. In other words, currently the legal assistant may have no legal secretarial skills as such.

Today, the legal assistant is increasingly likely to be a recent high school graduate who obtained his or her abilities and skills through a formal program of education or training.

CHAPTER XVII

Making Career Decisions

The field of legal assistant not only provides a variety of career opportunities but also the peace of mind of knowing that with proper initial and continuing education or training and with a job, you are virtually assured of continued or continuing employment there or elsewhere for as long as you may wish to work. From the preceding chapters, you have learned of the variety of specialized occupations and careers that are available. As a member of the legal services team, involved with the field of law as well as that of legal assistant, you will encounter many interesting circumstances as well as challenging legal questions, some of which will have import beyond particular facts. Because formal education or training for legal assistants is a comparatively new phenomenon, the great majority of legal assistants were at one time legal secretaries. Through observation and on-the-job training, these people advanced by promotions from positions as legal secretaries to careers as legal assistants. In this chapter, we shall discuss how a career as a legal assistant enables you to move laterally from a generalist to a specialist and from one particular specialty to another related or unrelated one.

As a matter of choice, you may prefer to remain in your initial position and make continued progress on the job. In the alternative, you may wish to use your legal assistant education and training as a springboard to a career directly or indirectly related to the field of law.

As mentioned in Chapter III, a number of men who later became Presidents of the U.S. had careers in law that began in humble fashion. Many other men and women who now occupy positions of high prestige in law firms, businesses, and governmental posts also began at the bottom of the ladder. Without formal education or training, they achieved success by acquiring reputations as being dedicated, reliable, and hard-working. Although the concept was not recognized as such at that time, some of these people were what would now be described as legal assistants. Others were in the nature of law clerks, a temporary status for today's law students, as discussed in Chapter I. Be that as it may, either or both of these methods of advancement was more likely to take place in the past. In general, legal assistants today usually have obtained their education or training through some formal course of instruction. Moreover, legal assistants do not as a matter of course advance to lawyer to judge. A career as a lawyer normally precedes that of a judge and requires education over and above that necessary for a career as a legal assistant.

These facts are important to you, because positions as legal assistants nevertheless do provide a means of entry although certainly not the only one, into a number of other careers, most of them related to the field of legal assistant but others distinctly separate. Examples of related employment might include a position with a commercial bank or trust department where not your legal assistant skills but your education or training would be useful in the creation and administration of trusts. Examples of employment distinctly separate from the field of legal assistant might include work in the office of an insurance or real estate broker who had recognized the need for a person with your particular abilities in meeting problems encountered in those fields.

Despite what may seem like greener pastures elsewhere, if you give the job you have your very best effort and gain the respect and support of your lawyer-employer and the other members of the legal services team, promotions and salary increases should be forthcoming. Realistically, how you will be able to perform on your first job is a secondary consideration. Your primary concern should be beginning your career under the best possible circumstances.

Your first employment will enable you to obtain experience. Experience provides opportunities either to move up in the legal assistant field or to branch out for career opportunities in other fields. A greater number of opportunities will be yours as the depth and breadth of your experience increase. Opportunities will also increase as the field of law itself expands. For the future, these factors should combine to increase the number of your career choices and the likelihood that you will be able, sooner or later, to find a position particularly suited to your personality and abilities, and at an appropriate level of compensation.

A legal assistant career offers differing employment opportunities plus the chance to serve society in a variety of ways. Every person in the U.S. will probably, at one time or another, have one or more legal problems. From resolution of one pressing problem it is a short step to a continuing client relationship involving planning the entire legal needs of a person. Your reputation for excellence in performance will help to build the organization of which you are a part.

What does this all mean for you? One, it means that your education or training for a legal assistant career combined with experience is a marketable commodity for legal assistant and other careers. Two, it means that obtaining your education or training required you to develop certain good habits that will stand you in good stead throughout your working lifetime— abilities to concentrate, think logically, and solve problems. Three, it means that experience on the job in a legal assistant career will give you useful knowledge about the world of work in general. The benefits of these three factors can be used and applied should your career shift to a different segment of the legal assistant field or another career entirely.

For legal assistants in particular, experience in one or more of the occupational specializations will increase their degree and extent of job mobility. The more education or training and experience you are able to acquire, the easier it will be to change employers and location. Although your movement will be somewhat restricted by the legal peculiarities of particular jurisdictions, even now and increasingly in the future as our society becomes more and more homogeneous you will be able to tap a national job market, especially if your specialty is one which is at that time in high demand.

CHAPTER XVIII

Appropriate Attitudes for a Legal Assistant Career

In Chapter I personality and abilities necessary for a successful legal assistant career were discussed. In this chapter, the related question of attitudes required for success as a legal assistant will be considered. Attitudes are emotions, feelings, or temperament, a predisposition or tendency to react or respond in one way or another to your environment, objects both animate and inanimate, and circumstances. The success or failure of your career as a legal assistant may depend on the appropriateness of your attitudes, which may ultimately be more crucial to your success than superior ability or sparkling personality.

You may be a legal assistant in the arctic or the tropics, in a law firm, corporation, or governmental agency. Whatever your physical location, whoever your employer may be, your attitudinal obligation is the same: to be "a professional." The expression: "She or he is a professional" connotes many responsibilities. Legal assistants cannot afford to be sensitive or irritable. You must be willing to subordinate your emotions to the needs of others—your employer and the client. Exercise judgment in your mode of dress as well as behavior.

Webster's New Collegiate Dictionary defines the word "professional" as meaning first, in three parts: "(a) of, relating to or characteristic of a profession; (b) engaged in one of the learned professions; (c) characterized by or conforming to the ethical standards of a profession"; second, in two parts, as: "(a) participating for gain or livelihood in an activity or field of endeavor often engaged in by amateurs; (b) engaged in by persons receiving financial return"; and third as: "following a line of conduct as though it were a profession."

The legal assistant is or should be a professional except for the fact that she or he is not engaged directly in one of the three professions traditionally considered the learned professions, law, medicine, and the clergy. Nevertheless, the legal assistant is directly involved in the field of law and the delivery of legal services. In every other sense of the word "professional" the activities of the legal assistant should meet its definition.

Because of the close working relationship between the lawyer and the legal assistant, what the legal assistant does should be characteristic of the spirit of the profession of law with which he or she is associated. As you will learn later, the legal assistant, in the opinion of one professional organization of legal assistants, should be governed not only by a code of ethical conduct for legal assistants but also by the same rules of professional conduct that bind lawyers. The legal assistant earns a livelihood from work as a legal assistant; in that sense, too, he or she is acting not as an amateur but as a professional. Finally, in the best sense of the phrase, the legal assistant is "following a line of conduct as though it were a profession." To coin an expression, "The zeal is real," for the work of a legal assistant, like that of a lawyer, affects "life, liberty, and the pursuit of happiness," not to mention rights to specific property.

Legal assistants who possess insight and a large degree of self-understanding will be most likely to be of the greatest assistance to their employers and clients. Will you assume responsibility for your own behavior even though your lawyer-employer will be ultimately responsible as well? Will you be self-reliant in the making of decisions? If you prefer to defer to others and rely on their judgment instead of your own, you would do well to examine your attitudes in this regard. Remember that for those in the field of legal assistant, the ultimate exercise of judgment is not always how to proceed but when to proceed. A clear division of tasks and responsibilities between the lawyer and the legal assistant will enhance both your self-reliance and the confidence of your employer in your abilities.

The legal services delivered by the team of which you will be a part will produce both short- and long-range results. Will you seek help in achieving proper results from other members of the team as well as the client and third parties? Do you look upon those who seek help as demonstrating weakness or ineptitude? Such an opinion may demonstrate your own attitude of insecurity. Be secure enough to seek help whenever and from whomever or wherever it may be available. Experience is the greatest if not the only teacher. Will you learn from what experience has to teach, gain from mistakes of the past, and change your approach for the future as required? Do you control your own life, or are you pushed about willy-nilly by the wills, wishes, and whims of others? Are you the kind of person who will plan and manage your education and career (high school, college, or legal assistant training program, job, and professional) advancement? Do you view yourself realistically? Do you accept your abilities and limitations? Will you do what is required by the circumstances you encounter? Will you be effective in obtaining and applying knowledge to solve problems?

Before you embark upon a legal assistant career, make certain that you do not need more help than those you will be trying to assist. Any personal problems you are experiencing are likely to be increased by exposure to the difficulties of others. The pressures of the job will be felt by some more than others. What will your reactions be? Will it frighten you to work with those who are alleged to be criminals? Can you interview a bereaved widow or a seriously injured person or his family without yourself being overcome with grief and sorrow? Will it absolutely kill you to keep a confidence disclosed by your employer or a client, to tell no one, not even your spouse or parents, what you may learn in secret during the course of your employment?

Not only will you be required to prove adequate in the face of the demands of a legal assistant career, but also you must be aware that your employer and the client will be relying upon you for your help to resolve the problems presented. Will you be able to respond when your employer makes what you consider to be excessive demands—when the client needs assistance but will not cooperate beyond a bare plea for help?

As far as investigative work is concerned, will you go out into the community or beyond to determine the facts that are necessary to help your employer or the client? You will find that office interviews will not always be adequate to develop the facts necessary to solve the problems presented.

Do you have or can you develop the patience necessary to involve clients significantly in efforts to assist themselves? Will you keep your head when interview techniques, the standard method of obtaining information from clients, are both challenging and laborious? These approaches, which are intended to inform and promote recognition of solutions to problems of clients, will test your mettle as well. Will you be able to accept and overcome initial helplessness or hopelessness of clients?

Operating as a professional, will you always be able to maintain a distance between yourself and clients, rejecting any impulse to guide, or more correctly misguide, them in one direction or the other for whatever selfish reasons? Will you keep the relationship between yourself and the client on a strictly professional basis?

If you are a member of a minority group, do you have a strength of purpose in your life, perseverance, and ability to adjust to misfortune or change? These qualities of character will be prerequisite to preparing for and joining the legal services team as a legal assistant. If you are given special consideration for admission to college or programs of training for legal assistants, if you are afforded the benefit of any doubt as to the quality of your coursework and helped to find your first employment, will your abilities but more particularly your attitudes be the equal of those of your fellow legal assistants who are not members of minority groups? Will you reject what may be a heritage of discrimination to gain balanced objectivity about yourself and your place in society, to strive for realizable achievements? As a member of the legal services team, will you keep and maintain your cultural background and heritage, your identity with the minority group of which you are a part, rejecting the options of becoming another one of the majority for all intents and purposes, or a professional zealot, or an exploitative money grubber?

Never let the temporary sameness of your daily activities blind you to the reality that each client has a unique problem insofar as he or she is concerned. Some clients may have more difficulties than you would care to imagine. You will need to provide understanding and sympathy whenever and wherever you can. Moreover, when the client needs help or is entangled in a seemingly hopeless web of difficulties, will you go the extra mile to find the facts or the point of law that may make the difference between success and failure? If a particular client's circumstances are the reflection of a societal problem, will you be willing to work to resolve the underlying causes, arousing public opinion, seeking to reverse an erroneous appellate court decision or to enact corrective legislation?

Before you embark upon a career as a legal assistant, decide for yourself whether your attitudes are appropriate. If they are not, you will be neither effective nor happy as a legal assistant, although your personality and abilities may be well suited to such a career. Make a decision as to the appropriateness of your attitudes before you begin your training; do not delay that assessment. To assist you in that determination, you are encouraged to examine the ethical codes reproduced in Appendices II A, B, and C before proceeding further.

CHAPTER XIX

Kinds of Legal Assistant Work

The vast majority of people who choose legal assistant careers will be employed by men or women who are engaged in the private practice of law. This figure will approach or perhaps exceed 70 percent of you who become employed as legal assistants. The remaining 30 percent will be divided between those employed by corporations or some other form of business organization and those employed in governmental work. Perhaps one-fourth of the remaining 30 percent will be employed by business and the balance in government. Legal assistants working for government, about one-fourth of the total of all legal assistants employed, may find themselves in any one of the three branches of government—executive, legislative, or judicial—and at various administrative agencies. Employment may be at any level of government, local or municipal, village, town or city, county, state, or federal.

The particular legal assistant abilities and skills that you will use on the job will be dictated in largest measure by the nature of your employer's practice. That, in turn, will be profoundly affected by whether he or she practices alone or with a group, by his or her educational background and experience, and his or her location.

One group of governmental occupations for the legal assistant is in the judicial branch of government. Most legal assistants so employed would work as clerks for judges at the county or state level. Others might be employed in the office of the Clerk of Courts, who has responsibility for maintaining the records of all litigation that is pending in the county. Another large group of governmental legal assistants would be employed principally at the county level in the offices of various officials: the Register of Deeds, the Registrar in Probate, or the Corporation Counsel.

Another major segment of governmental legal assistants would be employed in the administration of the criminal justice system —again principally at the county level in the office of the District or Prosecuting Attorney. The balance of legal assistants employed by government, a small fraction, would work in the offices of various regulatory agencies, mostly at the state level. Employment by such administrative agencies, while relatively small today, is perhaps the fastest-growing area of future employment for legal assistants, as the number of administrative agencies and the complexity of their regulations grows apace.

CHAPTER XX

The Key Professionals

As discussed in Chapter I, the legal services team consists of a minimum of three types of professionals: the lawyer, the legal assistant, and the legal secretary. Each of these three has significant and distinct contributions to make. Without each being present, there could be no team effort. The role of the legal assistant in its various aspects has been treated in depth throughout this book. The purpose of this chapter in general is to elaborate on the roles of the lawyer and the legal secretary. In particular, how the legal assistant interacts with them and how they interact with him or her to enhance the team effort will be discussed.

First, let us consider the interaction between the legal assistant and the lawyer to make a more productive team effort. Generally, the more information you as a legal assistant have about your lawyer-employer, the better off you and the team will be. In like manner, the lawyer who employs you will want to know as much as possible about you. The pre-law educational background of the lawyer is potentially varied. The vast majority of today's and tomorrow's lawyers and your potential employers will have obtained an undergraduate degree in some field of study. That field of study may have been one of the liberal arts, English, foreign languages, history, literature, or journalism. It may have been in one of the sciences, chemistry, physics, biology, or zoology. Many engineering backgrounds are also possible—aeronautical, civil, electrical, mechanical, and nuclear as examples. Business administration is another likely choice of pre-law students. Such persons may have majored in accounting, general business, economics, industrial relations, or marketing.

This variety of undergraduate backgrounds may have a more profound effect on the prospective lawyer's future than his course of instruction in law school.

The curriculum of law schools has traditionally remained the same over the decades. It is only recently, typically through the addition of seminars, that topics of current interest such as equal employment opportunity and natural resources law have been added. There still remain basic traditional law school courses usually taken during the first year. These courses may include business organizations, constitutional law, contracts, criminal law, personal and real property, and torts (private wrongs). It is only in the second and third years of law school that the student may take advanced courses that provide the detailed knowledge and information acquired by the legal assistant in the course of his or her education or training. This is particularly the case with respect to certain legal assistant specialties other than those practic·d by the criminal law specialist and the real estate or real property law specialist. The legal assistant specialties for which the lawyer obtains some of his training beyond the first year in law school include business or corporate law, estate work or probate law, and litigation.

Moreover, you should know that the emphasis of most law school education tends to be general and theoretical and not on the specifics or how to accomplish particular results. By way of contrast, the emphasis of your education or training is likely to be quite the opposite. You should be taught specifics and how to accomplish particular results. The general objectives of the instructors of each of your courses should be to give you some knowledge of the theory of the subject but only enough to help you know why the practice or practical aspects of the theory are as they are. Principally, you will be taught "how to do it" in the context of particular subjects. It is quite possible, therefore, that the lawyer who has employed you will seem less familiar with the practical aspects of how to accomplish specific tasks than you are. Nevertheless, the lawyer has the big picture, the legal theory, which you as the legal assistant will lack. Do not be disturbed by this; it is the way it was intended to be.

The legal assistant and the lawyer will work best together if the legal assistant keeps this knowledge in the forefront. The legal assistant, as his or her experience and knowledge increase, will be able to provide detailed information as to the facts or the law. Incorporating information as to the facts or the law that you as the legal assistant can provide with his or her general or specific knowledge, the lawyer can reach a sounder legal conclusion than could be reached otherwise. You and your lawyer-employer are capable of being a very efficient component of the legal services team, and clients will be better served.

The third essential member of the legal services team is the legal secretary. The legal secretary may well have obtained secretarial training from a community, junior, or technical college. Moreover, it is possible that this training will have been as a general secretary. The legal assistant, then, can be of great help to the new legal secretary who has no specific legal background. For example, as you will come to learn, the law is a language unto itself. And each area of the law has its own particular language. The legal assistant can be of great assistance to the secretary in teaching her words with which she may not be familiar. In addition, do not fail to take advantage of what the legal secretary can teach you about the idiosyncrasies of the law office or legally related activity in which you become employed, not to mention the specific person or people who have employed you or for whom you will be working.

You and the legal secretary can be potentially the best of friends or the worst of enemies. You should do all within your power to see that it is the former. The same philosophy holds true for other legal assistants in the office. As your knowledge and experience grow, the lawyer may some day make you responsible for supervising the legal secretary and other legal assistants. It is also possible that sometime during your career you will be supervised by another legal assistant. Whatever your circumstances at any given moment, you, other legal assistants, and the legal secretary are also capable of being very efficient components of the legal services team.

In summary, the legal assistant is the legal services team's person in the middle, between the lawyer above and the legal secretary below. In either direction, upward or downward, the personality, abilities and skills, and attitudes of the legal assistant can accentuate or diminish the success of the legal services team.

CHAPTER XXI

Group Legal Services

In a book of this nature, some consideration should be given to a description of current or emerging trends likely to have the greatest effects in the foreseeable future on your occupational choice. At the moment perhaps the strongest such trend that will affect the use of lawyers and legal assistants are plans to provide group legal services or group plans. Group plans are also sometimes called prepaid legal services plans.

Many lawyers either fear or actively oppose the emergence of this phenomenon. There are potentially good reasons for such fears or objections—ethical considerations, antitrust implications, and questions regarding taxation of benefits and insurance regulations.

Ethical considerations and antitrust implications were also matters of concern with respect to whether or not lawyers should be permitted to advertise. The Supreme Court of the United States has held that restrained advertising by lawyers is to be considered both ethically and legally proper. Both group plans and lawyer advertising should have profound effects on the amount and nature of the work available to lawyers. Some of this work can be properly accomplished by trained legal assistants. In fact, in some cases, it may be uneconomic for the client to insist that certain tasks be performed by the lawyer himself.

Two types of group plans are available. One is the so-called closed panel plan. Under this version, one law firm in a given geographical area will provide all necessary legal services included under the terms of the plan to all members of the group and their families. A second type of plan is the so-called open panel plan. The open panel may include all persons licensed to practice law in a given geographical area.

The group may consist of any assemblage of persons capable of being recognized as such. It could be teachers, city workers, other professionals such as doctors or dentists, or members of particular unions such as the carpenters or teamsters.

As the concept would indicate, all legal services are rendered by the firm to members of the group and their families pursuant to the plan. Both services to be provided and rates to be charged would be specified within the plan. Services might include family law matters, real estate and tenant problems, collections and civil litigation, estate planning and probate matters, retail credit problems and bankruptcy, and municipal court matters. Rates charged would vary with the services to be rendered.

The plan would also contain certain exclusions and limitations, among which might be: (1) matters not of a personal nature—in other words, legal questions arising out of the operation of a business enterprise by a member of the plan; (2) criminal matters—where the person is charged with a serious crime or subject to being fined or penalized; (3) matters covered by insurance; (4) preparation of individual income tax returns; (5) matters related to a member's employment; and (6) legal actions begun before the effective date of the plan.

You can see that there are many areas in which the legal assistant generalist could be utilized. Opportunities also exist for the estate work or probate law specialist, the litigation specialist, and the real estate or real property law specialist. Other legal assistant specialists not specifically discussed in this book could find work as well. These would certainly include the domestic relations or family law specialist and the credit and collection or commercial law specialist.

CHAPTER XXII

Pro Bono Publico Work

"Pro bono publico" is a Latin phrase meaning "for the public good or welfare." For lawyers, it means work that they perform —legal services—for the benefit of the public. Lawyers sometimes abbreviate the expression to "pro bono work." A discussion of pro bono work is provided here because of the important role that legal assistants can play with respect to it.

All services that lawyers render are or should be for the benefit of the public, or at least those members of the public who are their clients at any given time. But pro bono work is a larger concept than this. It means legal services rendered to serve mankind in general. Lawyers, as well as legal assistants and other working members of society, certainly have a right to earn a respectable living. All that either the lawyer or the legal assistant has to sell is his or her knowledge, time, and effort. Sometimes the expenses of rendering legal services, rent, wages and salaries, and utilities, will exceed the amount that can be reasonably charged for these services. At other times, expenses of rendering legal services will exceed the ability of a client or clients to pay.

Despite either one of these two circumstances, the legal community continues to believe in its professional obligation to assist those members of society who cannot afford to pay in proportion to the cost of the services rendered or who perhaps cannot afford to pay at all. This is the essence of the philosophy of pro bono work. Either of these two circumstances often provides opportunities for legal assistants. Lawyers can utilize their legal assistants under supervision to perform certain kinds of pro bono work that they could not afford to perform themselves.

You as legal assistants will find the questions presented to be no less challenging or interesting merely because they cannot be performed on an economic basis.

CHAPTER XXIII

Financing Your Legal Assistant Education or Training

You may well be worried about how you will be able to finance your legal assistant education or training. Your parents will be equally concerned about how to pay for as little as two years of education beyond high school at a community, junior, or technical college or as many as five years for a four-year liberal arts college degree followed by an additional period of legal assistant training.

A community, junior, or technical college education is the least expensive of the available alternatives. Although the costs of food and lodging will vary depending upon where you obtain your education or training, perhaps the larger variable is the cost of tuition. The cost of tuition at a community, junior, or technical college will be a small fraction of the expense at a state university. The possibility of living and eating at home if you attend a community, junior, or technical college will further reduce the cost of this alternative.

Attending a four-year college will, of course, be more costly than a community, junior, or technical college education. Not only will tuition per semester or per quarter be higher at an institution offering a baccalaureate degree, but the time required will be twice as long. The possibility of obtaining your education while living at home may also be less. Any way you look at it, four years of college is an expensive proposition.

Worse yet, private four-year colleges, some of which are considered more prestigious than state-supported institutions, are even more expensive. If your plans do not include education or training as a legal assistant within your college curriculum, additional expense, not to mention time, will be incurred to obtain the specific training. Continuing inflation will make high costs today even higher tomorrow. Should there be more than one child in your family who will require higher education during the same period of time, your family's financial problems will be compounded.

Despite this potential bad news, there is a ray of sunshine. Financial aid from several sources—governmental, institutional, and private—is increasing faster than the expenses of college, according to the College Board, a nonprofit association to aid opportunities for higher education. In 1979 it is estimated that academic costs will increase 6 percent over the preceding year; however, state and federal funds for financial aid are expected to increase 15 percent. The College Board expects funds for financial aid from all sources to reach $12.3 billion nationally in 1979.

President Carter has discussed tax credits to parents of college students in addition to the expansion of programs of financial aid to students that are presently available. You should explore and take advantage of these financial aids. You may be able to put together a package of scholarships, loans, and part-time jobs that will entirely free your parents from financing your education or training as a legal assistant. Even students from so-called middle-income families may be eligible for several kinds of aid.

The availability of scholarships has changed over the years. Traditionally those that were available were academic scholarships, awarded only to the brightest students. Even today a high school student who is in the top 10 percent of his or her class should be able to find an academic scholarship. There are other academic scholarships, such as the National Merit Scholarships. Some service clubs, national organizations with local affiliates, offer scholarships based in whole or in part on academic achievement in high school.

In the 1960's societal concerns with the plight of the disadvantaged had an effect on the availability of scholarships. The emphasis shifted from awarding scholarships purely on the basis of academic excellence to one of need. Now, giving consideration to both academic excellence and need as well as other demonstrated ability, scholarships are available for athletes, musicians, those interested in law enforcement, and others. Given your interest in a career as a legal assistant, you will want to check with the financial aid office of the program of education or training in which you are interested. You will also want to check with your high school as to the availability of local scholarships.

Today, for the vast majority of scholarships, need must be established. Several factors are considered in establishing need. Family income level is perhaps the most important but not the only factor. Other considerations include the size of the family and the number of children in college. Applying these criteria to particular facts, a family of four with an annual income of $15,000 and one child pursuing higher education might expect to meet federal requirements for funds to cover part of the academic expenses. One of the newest and largest federal programs is the Basic Educational Opportunity Grant. Grants ranging from $50 to $1,400 per year are based on need. Federal money is also available under the Supplemental Educational Opportunity Grant. Special scholarships or grants may be available to those in special circumstances.

If scholarship money is not available, and you believe in yourself and your present abilities or those you can acquire, do not hesitate to obtain a loan. In addition, you may consider getting a job in the community. A job may not only provide you with the money necessary to complete your education, but it also may enable you to gain valuable experience and even permanent employment following graduation.

CHAPTER XXIV

Opportunities for Everyone

The decade of the 1960's brought civil rights to the forefront of public concern. The increasing impatience of the disadvantaged caused both the public and private sectors to acknowledge that discrimination in employment and other circumstances on the basis of sex, race, religion, age, and physical condition would no longer be tolerated. In the 1970's equal employment opportunity is the watchword. There are lawyers who specialize in equal employment opportunity law. It is also possible for legal assistants to be equal employment opportunity law specialists. Members of groups that have suffered or continue to suffer from discriminatory practices may be particularly interested in these opportunities.

To the discredit of the legal profession and perhaps society at large, the rights of owners of property have traditionally taken precedence over concern for people. Fortunately, in more recent times the law itself has been a prominent vehicle in giving expression to social concerns. As a result, new dimensions have been added to the fields of both law and legal assistant. Clients whose legal needs have never been met before are now being helped by the legal services team.

Opportunities for Women—and Men

As mentioned in the Introduction, women clearly outnumber men both in employment statistics and in numbers enrolled in programs of education or training for legal assistants. If you are a man, do not be concerned about the statistical probability that a legal assistant will be a woman. There are rewarding opportunities for men in the field of legal assistant just as men have found satisfying careers as nurses, a field in which there are also greater numbers of women than men. Do not be dismayed by an interviewer who is really looking for a legal secretary and not a legal assistant. Seek an employer who will use your unique personality, abilities and skills, and attitudes. Certain potential employers may find male applicants preferable for positions in particular legal assistant specialties. Examples might include the specialty in criminal law and certain subspecialties in civil litigation such as the investigator. Men who choose careers as legal assistants may be drawn to those same specialties for which potential employers might prefer them, as the examples above may indicate.

Opportunities for the Disadvantaged

Perhaps the greatest disadvantage in this world is an economic one, although economic disadvantage may be strongly related to minority group status. Nevertheless, those who are economically disadvantaged have several distinct advantages if they choose the field of legal assistant as a career. First, those who could not otherwise afford to finance their education or training as legal assistants may receive financial help while seeking to enter the field of legal assistant. Such help is available through CETA, the federal Comprehensive Employment and Training Act of 1973. For some of you, other educational benefits are available, such as those from the Veterans Administration. Second, as discussed in Chapter XV, there are financial rewards for those who enter the legal assistant field. Third, the disadvantaged may find job satisfaction—beyond mere financial reward—as discussed in Chapter X. And this satisfaction may be felt more deeply by the disadvantaged than by those who are not.

Members of Minority Groups

The U.S. is predominantly a nation of comparatively recent immigrants and their progeny. Most of these left their native lands, more or less voluntarily, to seek new lives in America. Negro slaves brought from Africa were a distinct exception. Their struggle for freedom and to overcome a number of obstacles—including the concept of "separate but equal" in the field of education and elsewhere—has been a long and enduring one. Much of the progress that has been accomplished thus far and will surely come took place or will take place as the result of application or reexamination of legal principles as they affect the Negro. Members of this and other minority races may find more individual job satisfaction as legal assistants who are equal employment opportunity law specialists than in many other specialties.

As America became populated with immigrants from Europe and other continents, the native American Indians were, in some cases, brutally pushed aside. Relocated to reservations and deprived of their means of livelihood, many—some quietly, some less so—lost or were deprived of their self-respect. Equal employment opportunity law is only one, then, of the potential job responsibilities of the American Indian law specialist. Property rights, as well as human rights, have been, are, and will be at issue. But, like the Negro who becomes a legal assistant specializing in the law governing employment opportunities for members of his race, the legal assistant who is an American Indian has the opportunity, in choosing to specialize in the legal concerns of these peoples, to obtain job satisfaction not available in other positions.

In summary, you are unique, whether you will be the so-called typical legal assistant—a comparatively young woman—or one of many who each may be statistically atypical. Whatever your individual circumstances, recognize your uniqueness and use it to your advantage. If that be your choice as one who has been disadvantaged or is a member of a minority group, use your new-found abilities and skills to help those similarly situated. In so doing, you will help yourself and society as well.

CHAPTER XXV

Sources for Securing Jobs, Your Résumé, and Personal Interviews

How can you put your best foot forward in securing the position you desire? Before beginning an active search, you should already have made some important preliminary decisions. You should have decided whether you want to be a generalist or a specialist and why, and if your choice is a specialty, the particular specialty in which you wish to engage and why. You should know the geographical area and perhaps the particular community in which you wish to work. You should know something about the nature of each of your potential employers—law firms, corporations, agencies, branches, departments or offices of government—and, in general, the objectives of each organization. It is fine to be certain about a number of things that will have a profound effect on the course of your career, but you should remain flexible as long as possible before making your final employment decision. Allow your original preference to be subject to change in the event that an advantage you did not expect becomes available to you. Do not solidify your career thinking too early.

Make your search for a legal assistant position known to everyone who might be of help to you—members of your immediate family, relatives, friends, neighbors, teachers, and fellow students. In doing so, give them as much information about your background and career goals as they seem able or willing to absorb. Someone you talk to may have a piece of information you would not have obtained otherwise—a vacancy of which you were unaware or the name of someone to call for an interview appointment.

You will be most likely to obtain your first position through the placement facilities of the educational institution or program of training of which you are a graduate. Once you have or are beyond your first position as a legal assistant, local or national professional organizations and word-of-mouth will be sources of information concerning new or different positions. Professional organizations are also good sources of jobs for those who have no association or no immediate past association with a particular educational institution or program of training. You will want to join one or more of such organizations if for no other reason than because of the job information they can provide. Two of these professional organizations are The National Association of Legal Assistants, Inc., 3005 East Skelly Drive, Suite 120, Tulsa, Oklahoma 74105; and The National Federation of Paralegal Associations, Ben Franklin Station, P.O. Box 14103, Washington, D.C. 20044. As the field of Legal Assistant continues to grow, additional organizations may be formed. In addition, do not discount the help you may obtain from fellow members or from publications of school or local professional organizations of legal assistants.

Because you will be seeking employment in a field directly related to law, it is also possible to obtain employment through professional organizations or publications of lawyers. You may wish to advertise your availability for employment in the publications of these professional organizations and the classified advertising sections of the newspapers.

You may wish to register with a fee-charging agency. In doing so, make certain of the terms and conditions under which you will owe a fee to the agency. If the fee is payable whether or not you obtain suitable employment as a result of its efforts, you should look elsewhere. In any event, reach an agreement on the charges that will be due in advance. These charges are often a stipulated fraction of your first year's income. Good agencies often render valuable services.

If you live, go to school, or work in the same area in which you wish to find your first position or to change jobs, do not hesitate to visit as many as possible of the employers in the area. On rare occasions, you may find a situation in which a need for a person with your training and abilities has arisen due to growth of the workload, the addition of one or more lawyers or legal specialties, or the recent resignation of a legal assistant.

From time to time, professional organizations sponsor state, regional, and national conventions, each a combination of social activity and continuing education on one or perhaps a number of subjects of interest. Even though your pocket or purse may be stretched to the breaking point, such a trip may be a worthwhile investment, particularly if you are in the market for a new or different position. At such conventions, potential employers are where you find them. They may be found at business meetings, dinner or luncheon engagements, or social events. Even if no job interviews result from the convention experience, you will in a short time have obtained a concentrated education in a legal assistant field of your interest. Looking on the bright side, however, in addition to whatever informal contacts you may be able to make, formal arrangements may have been made by the sponsor of the convention to allow prospective employers and legal assistants to conduct employment interviews during the convention.

If none of the job-finding techniques already discussed are available to you, a direct-mail campaign can be conducted no matter what your educational or personal circumstances. To begin a direct mail campaign, compile a list of potential employers in the fields of law or legal assistant in geographical areas or communities where you would be most willing to accept employment. Consult a current edition of the *Martindale-Hubbell Law Directory,* a five-volume set that lists lawyers by states with their professional associations and descriptions of their practices. For legal assistants interested in working for lawyers engaged in particular specialties, other legal directories are available, such as *The Lawyer to Lawyer Consultation Panel,* which lists lawyers by states and areas of specialization. Consult the library or placement office of your educational institution or training program. The law librarian of the college or school of law nearest you may offer additional assistance. Besides published directories, telephone books and professional journals of lawyers and legal assistants are additional sources of information in the making of a list of persons, firms, corporations, or governmental organizations to which you can apply for employment.

Your Résumé—The Essence of You

Your résumé and covering letter are your opportunities to precede yourself. Well conceived and well written, your résumé and accompanying letter not only gain personal interviews but also sell you before you have the opportunity to sell yourself. They represent a "condensed you." They are the keys to your first job and probably every job you will ever have. They are together a traveling composite of your personality and abilities, your attitudes, experience, vital statistics, and references as to character and previous employment.

Can you make the essence of you in each and in all of these respects fit into a résumé of one or at most two pages of pure information? Not only does your résumé serve the fundamental purpose of providing all the relevant information about you, but it puts that information in one convenient place capable of being retrieved on a moment's notice.

The résumé itself should be an impersonal recitation of the biographical information indicated in general above. The cover or transmittal letter is your second opportunity to give your potential employer some insight into you as a person and how your particular attitudes, abilities, and background of training and experience could be of particular assistance to him or her.

There are as many opinions on how best to write a résumé as there are people looking for positions as legal assistants. Optimally, the information provided by the résumé when typed single-spaced with generous margins should fit comfortably on a single sheet of paper. The information should be specific and include the same information that would be provided by a standard application for employment. Included, among other information, should be the following: (1) name and address; (2) positions previously held; (3) dates of prior employment; (4) names and addresses of former employers and/or supervisors; (5) educational or training history with dates of all certificates, diplomas, and degrees awarded; (6) names, addresses, telephone numbers, and relationships of particular references.

A good résumé is divided into sections including the information given above, usually arranged in the form of a block outline, perhaps as follows:

TITLE OF RÉSUMÉ (For example, centered at the top of the page: "Personal Résumé of (your first name, middle initial, and last name)".

ADDRESS AND TELEPHONE NUMBER (Provide more than one telephone number, if necessary. Be certain you or someone can be reached regularly and without difficulty at one or more of the numbers given.)

CAREER GOALS (Insert a very brief description of your career objectives, short-term and long-term. For example, as a practicing legal assistant, do you wish to be a generalist or a specialist? If you wish to be a specialist, what particular specialty is your career goal?)

EDUCATIONAL HISTORY (Include descriptions with dates of all certificates, diplomas, and degrees awarded. Also include any awards or scholarships and honors received, including your grade point average or class rank, if available.)

MILITARY, ALTERNATE, OR PUBLIC SERVICE (If applicable, include information as to branch and dates of service, rank at entry and upon discharge, awards and medals, and particular duties, if any, providing experience applicable to a legal assistant career. Other possibilities for this category are alternate or noncombatant service, or public service such as the Peace Corps or VISTA. Do not be disturbed if you have no information to include that relates to this category. For military service, simply state: "No military or alternate service," giving the reason. If public service is not applicable, do not mention it.)

EMPLOYMENT HISTORY (Include positions previously held, dates of employment, etc. Begin with your most recent employment and work backward in time to the first position you held. Explanations should be provided for any gaps in your employment history, including, for example, education or training, and military, alternate, or public service. If the title of the position does not clearly reflect its duties, explain further, but succinctly. Give beginning and ending salary for each position held.)

EXTRACURRICULAR ACTIVITIES (Include here activities, hobbies, and sports in which you participate. Place special emphasis on those tending to increase your skills in oral and written communications.)

PERSONAL INFORMATION (Include your vital statistics such as your age or date of birth, place of birth or nationality, social security number, marital status, children if any, height, weight, state of health, and physical disabilities, if any.)

PERSONAL AND EMPLOYMENT REFERENCES (Provide the names, occupations, addresses, and telephone numbers of several persons who have agreed to serve as references for you. Indicate in each case whether their knowledge is personal or with respect to your past or present employment. Always ask permission to give a person's name as a reference. If someone agrees to serve as a reference, make complying with the request as easy as possible without interfering with the opportunity of the reference to be candid. Avoid repeated requests to the same persons by having reference letters sent to a central location such as the placement office of your school or training program or an employment agency. From this central location, photocopies can be distributed as needed. Never allow letters of reference to pass through your hands. Arrange to reimburse persons who have served as references for any expenses they may have incurred.)

Although there are differing views on the proper format or organization for a résumé, all are agreed that each résumé should be at best a typed original, as an unavoidable alternative, a crisp, clear photocopy of an original. Although a photocopy of a résumé may be an unavoidable alternative, *never* use a form letter for the cover letter.

Most employers will not consider a résumé and cover letter as substitutes for your completing a formal application for employment. Do not despair, for a good résumé will contain all the information required by the application. Use your résumé to make certain that you complete the application accurately.

Your Covering Letter

In most cases your résumé will be only an enclosure with that other most important part of your search for employment, the cover letter. Dedicate your efforts to creating for each position you seek the best possible cover letter. Although both the résumé and the letter can be tailored to meet particular circumstances, the letter will afford you the most latitude to emphasize those abilities and skills or that part of your educational background or training likely to be of greatest interest to one prospective employer or another. Nevertheless, the creation of a standard cover letter to accompany a standard résumé will serve as a vehicle for general inquiries concerning employment and as a working model for adaptation to particular job prospects.

Endeavor to address your letter to a single person and to insure that it and the enclosed résumé will be read and considered. Increase the likelihood of gaining the proper attention for your correspondence by doing the following: One, address by name and title, if available, the person who will make the employment decision, if you are able to identify him or her. Two, try to give the letter and résumé the appearance of being uniquely written for the particular position for which you are applying. Your letter and résumé are your sales tools; they have the unique ability to go where you cannot go without a formal invitation. Use this advantage wisely and in your own best interests. Make your letter and résumé clear, complete, concise, and above all, correct in all respects—grammar, punctuation, and spelling (abbreviate words sparingly, if at all). A lack of completeness as to the details of your education or training and experience or other important factors may subsequently result in your dismissal. A lack of correctness reflects on the written communication skills that are so important to your success as a practicing legal assistant.

Organize your search for employment by keeping lists of contacts you have made and responses you have received. A follow-up letter is appropriate if you have received no response to your initial inquiry within two weeks. Examine carefully the substance of the responses you do receive. Do what is requested, as applicable. For example, if you are asked for additional information or references, supply them as soon as possible. If you are invited to call or are called for a personal interview, make arrangements for it at your earliest mutual convenience. A lack of replies to your inquiries or questions or comments you receive may indicate that a revision of your letter or résumé is in order. Revise each as necessary, and keep trying for that all-important interview.

The Personal Interview

All the time and effort that preceded the personal interview was prelude. At the conclusion of the personal interview, or as soon as your qualifications and the results of your interview can be compared with those of other applicants, you will either be offered employment or not. Despite your training and abilities, whether or not you will have a career as a legal assistant in any particular position will ultimately depend on the results of the personal interview. You would be wise, therefore, to prepare yourself for each interview to the best of your ability. Concentrate your efforts toward the success of the personal interview.

Consider the following game plan in preparing for a personal interview. One, learn as much as possible about both the position and the person who will interview. Two, dress as you think you would be expected to dress if you were already employed in the position you are seeking; be prompt, but do not be distressed if the interviewer is not. Three, remember that the interviewer has something you want—a position as a legal assistant, and you have something he or she wants—the personality, abilities, skills, attitudes, and education or training that will make you a valuable employee. In this regard, make certain the interviewer understands that you have confidence in your abilities and that the position available is one that you will perform ably. Be as calm and relaxed as possible. Be open and candid in response to questions, and be certain you understand the question asked before you respond. If in doubt about what the questioner is seeking, do not hazard a guess. Ask a specific question in order to obtain the additional information necessary to frame an appropriate answer. Be prepared to respond to certain questions that may seem difficult to answer, including, of course, the question of salary; do not ask for more than you are prepared to accept.

CHAPTER XXVI

The Future of Your Future: Accreditation and Approval, Certification and Licensure

It seems an appropriate way to end this book by discussing the future of your future. Most of you will probably choose a formal course of instruction, rather than rely solely on on-the-job training. The future of your future will probably be affected most profoundly by the quality of the education or training you receive. The concepts of accreditation and approval and certification and licensure are indirect or direct ways in which legal assistants or those seeking to become legal assistants may be recognized. This recognition will be assisted or hindered by the quality of your education or training. As mentioned in Chapter I, the difficulty in obtaining such recognition is compounded by the lack of an acceptable or adequate definition of the occupation of legal assistant.

The first two of these four concepts, accreditation and approval, are indirect ways in which legal assistants or those seeking to become legal assistants may be recognized as such. Accreditation and approval each relate to educational institutions offering programs of instruction for legal assistants or to the programs of instruction themselves, not to the persons participating in the programs. Hence the term "indirect." With respect to accreditation, for example, Lakeshore Technical Institute, Cleveland, Wisconsin, whose Legal Assistant Course Program is discussed elsewhere in this book, is accredited by the North Central Association of Colleges and Secondary Schools, the Commission on Colleges and Universities. The process of receiving accreditation began with an application by the Institute in 1969, followed by the construction of a new campus and a five-year self-study, and culminated in a final on-site evaluation by a team from the North Central Association of Colleges and Secondary Schools, the Commission on Colleges and Universities, and subsequent accreditation. Accreditation, then, is a procedure by which an educational institution or course of instruction is evaluated and recognized by some agency or organization. The strength or value of the accreditation depends, in turn, on the stature or reputation of the accrediting agency.

Approval is usually approval of the course of instruction, not the educational institution itself. In some cases, however, the course of instruction and the educational institution that offers it may be one and the same. Again, the strength or value of the approval depends on the stature or reputation of the approving agency or organization. Approval by the American Bar Association of Legal Assistant Education Programs, for example, has been both praised and condemned. Individual judgments must be exercised on the appropriateness and quality of the standards applied in granting or withholding such approval.

The second two of these four concepts, certification and licensure, are direct ways in which legal assistants or those seeking to become legal assistants may be recognized as such. Certification and licensure relate to persons, legal assistants, not to educational institutions or to programs of instruction. Hence the term "direct." The concept of "Certified Legal Assistant" has been developed by the National Association of Legal Assistants, Inc. Information as to the examination that must be successfully completed to earn the designation as well as other activities of the association is available from The National Association of Legal Assistants, Inc., 3005 East Skelly Drive, Suite 122, Tulsa, Oklahoma 74105.

The State Bar of Oregon has a certification program for legal assistants. The State Bar of California and the Illinois State Bar Association have considered proposals for certifying legal assistants. Certification, then, is evaluation and recognition of individual achievement by nongovernmental or quasi-governmental organizations or agencies involved in the field of legal assistant.

Examples of licensure abound. In all states persons are required to be licensed to engage in a number of occupations and professions. These include accountants, barbers and beauticians, doctors, and lawyers. Licensure, then, is evaluation and recognition by a governmental agency of a certain level of competence possessed by a person in an occupation or profession. A strong trend toward the licensing of legal assistants has not yet taken hold. Again, perhaps this is largely due to the struggle toward definition discussed earlier, a battle you may help to win.

Institutions Offering Legal Assistant Education Programs, February, 1978

ALABAMA
Samford University
Adult Education
Birmingham, AL 35209

Spring Hill College
Paralegal Education Pgm.
Mobile, AL 36608

University of South Alabama
Div. of C.E. & Evening Studies
307 University Blvd.
Mobile, AL 36688

ALASKA
University of Alaska-Anchorage
Anchorage Community College
Law Science Program
2533 Providence Avenue
Anchorage, AK 99501

ARIZONA
Academy for Legal Assistants & Paralegals
Luhrs Central Building
Suite L
132 S. Central Avenue
Phoenix, AZ 85003

Northern Arizona University
Legal Assistant Program
Box 15066
Flagstaff, AZ 86011

Paralegal Institute (The)
3201 N. 16th St., Ste. 11
Phoenix, AZ 85016

Phoenix College
Department of Business
1202 West Thomas Road
Phoenix, AZ 85013

Scottsdale Community College
Pima and Chaparral Roads
P.O. Box Y
Scottsdale, AZ 85252

Sterling School
1010 East Indian Road
Phoenix, AZ 85014

CALIFORNIA
American College of Paramedical Arts & Sciences
1800 North Broadway
Santa Ana, CA 92706

American Legal Services Institute
2719 Canada Boulevard
Glendale, CA 91208

American River College
4700 College Oak Drive
Sacramento, CA 95841

California College of Paralegal Studies
6832 Van Nuys Blvd.
Van Nuys, CA 91405

California State College
San Bernardino
Paralegal Studies
Dept. of Political Science
550 State College Parkway
San Bernardino, CA 92407

California State University, Chico
Chico, CA 95929

California State University at Los Angeles
5151 State University Drive
Los Angeles, CA 90032

Canada College
4200 Farm Hill Boulevard
Redwood City, CA 94061

Cerritas College
11110 East Alondra Blvd.
Norwalk, CA 90650

City College of San Francisco
51 Phelan Avenue
San Francisco, CA 94112

Dominican College of San Rafael
San Rafael, CA 94901

Empire College
37 Old Court House Square
Santa Rosa, CA 95404

Fresno City College
1101 East University Ave.
Fresno, CA 93741

Golden West College
15744 Golden West
Huntington Beach, CA 92647

Humphreys College
6650 Inglewood Drive
Stockton, CA 92507

Imperial Valley College
P.O. Box 158
Imperial, CA 92251

Lone Mountain College
Graduate Legal Studies Program
2800 Turk Boulevard
San Francisco, CA 94118

Los Angeles City College
855 N. Vermont Avenue
Los Angeles, CA 90029

Los Angeles Southwest College
Legal Assistant
1600 West Imperial Highway
Los Angeles, CA 90047

Merritt College
12500 Campus Drive
Oakland, CA 94619

Orange Coast College
2701 Fairview Road
Costa Mesa, CA 92626

Pasadena City College
Business Department
1570 E. Colorado Blvd.
Pasadena, CA 91106

Pepperdine University
Legal Studies Program
8035 Vermont Avenue
Los Angeles, CA 90044

San Francisco City College
San Francisco, CA 94112

San Francisco State University Continuing Education/Extension
Paralegal Studies Program
1600 Holloway Avenue
San Francisco, CA 94132

Santa Ana College
Seventeenth at Bristol
Santa Ana, CA 92706

Sawyer College of Business
6832 Van Nuys Blvd.
Van Nuys, CA 91405

Skyline College
Paralegal Program
3300 College Drive
San Bruno, CA 94066

St. Mary's College
P.O. Box 52
Moraga, CA 94575

University of California at Berkeley
University Extension
2223 Fulton Street
Berkeley, CA 94720

Univ. of California-Irvine
Certificate Pgm. in Lgl. Asst.
Irvine, CA 92717

UCLA Extension
Attorney Assistant Tng. Pgm.
10995 LeConte Ave., Ste. 214
Los Angeles, CA 90024

University of San Diego
Lawyer's Assistant Program
Room 318, Serra Hall
Alcala Park
San Diego, CA 92110

University of Santa Clara
Institute for Paralegal Education
Bannan Hall, Room 261
Santa Clara, CA 95053

University of La Verne
1950 Third St.
La Verne, CA 91750

Univ. of Southern California
Program for Legal Paraprofessionals
Law Center
University Park
Los Angeles, CA 90007

University of West Los Angeles
School of Paralegal Studies
10811 Washington Blvd.
Culver City, CA 90230

West Valley College
1400 Fruitvale Avenue
Saratoga, CA 95070

COLORADO
Arapahoe Community College
Assoc. Degree Lgl. Asst. Pgm.

5900 S. Santa Fe Drive
Littleton, CO 80120

Colorado Paralegal Institute
609 W. Littleton Blvd., Ste. 306
Littleton, CO 80120

Community College of Denver
Auraria Campus
Service Occupations Division
Room CA-313
1111 W. Colfax
Denver, CO 80204

Denver Paralegal Institute, Ltd.
908 Central Bank West
1108—15th Street
Denver, CO 80202

El Paso Community College
2200 Bott Street
Colorado Springs, CO 80904

Southern Colorado State College
Behavioral & Social Sciences
900 W. Ormon
Pueblo, CO 81001

University of Denver
College of Law
Pgm. of Adv. Prof. Development
200 W. 14th Avenue
Denver, CO 80204

CONNECTICUT
Hartford College
Counseling Center for Women

1283 Asylum Avenue
Hartford, CT 06105

Manchester Community College
Box 1046
Manchester, CT 06040

Mattatuck Cmty. College
Legal Assistant Program
640 Chase Parkway
Waterbury, CT 06708

Norwalk Community College
333 Wilson Ave.
Route 136
Norwalk, CT 06854

Post College
Legal Assistant Program
800 Country Club Road
Waterbury, CT 06708

Quinnipiac College
Legal Assistant Program
Mount Carmel Avenue
Hamden, CT 06518

Sacred Heart University
P.O. Box 6460
Bridgeport, CT 06606

DELAWARE
Goldey Beacom College
Pike Creek Valley Campus
P.O. Box 5047
Wilmington, DE 19808

Wesley College
Dover, DE 19901

DISTRICT OF COLUMBIA
Antioch School of Law
Legal Technician Program
1624 Crescent Pl., N.W.
Washington, DC 20009

Georgetown University
School for Summer & C.E.
Legal Assistant Program
Washington, DC 20057

George Washington University
CEW Ctr.-College of Gnl. Stds.
2130 H St., N.W.-Ste. 621
Washington, D.C., 20052

Southeastern University
501 Eye Street, S.W.
Washington, DC 20006

FLORIDA
Florida Atlantic University
Institute for Lgl. Assts.
Center for Management & Professional Discipline
Boca Raton, FL 33431

Florida Technological University
Allied Legal Services Program
P.O. Box 25000
Orlando, FL 32816

Hillsborough Community College
P.O. Box 22127
Tampa, FL 33622

Langley Paralegal Institute
315 Hyde Park Avenue
Tampa, FL 33606

Manatee Junior College
P.O. Box 1849
Bradenton, FL 33506

Miami Dade Community College
Legal Assistant Program
300 N.E. 2nd Ave.
Miami, FL 33312

Santa Fe Community College
P.O. Box 1530
Gainesville, FL 32601

Southern Career Institute
1580 N.W. 2nd Avenue
Boca Raton, FL 33432

St. Petersburg Jr. College
Paralegal Program
P.O. Box 13489
St. Petersburg, FL

Valencia Community College
East Campus
P.O. Box 3028
Orlando, FL 32802

GEORGIA
Institute of Paralegal Tng.
c/o Columbia Southern College of Law of Georgia, Ltd.
4544 Memorial Drive
Decatur, GA 30032

Natl. Ctr. for Paralegal Tng.
Suite 430
3376 Peachtree Road, N.E.
Atlanta, GA 30326

HAWAII
Kapiolani Community College
Legal Assistant Program
620 Pensacola Street
Honolulu, HI 96814

ILLINOIS
MacCormac Junior College
327 S. LaSalle Street
Chicago, IL 60604

Mallinckrodt College
Legal Assistant Program
1041 Ridge Road
Wilmette, IL 60091

Midstate College
Paralegal Management
244 S.W. Jefferson
Peoria, IL 61602

Roosevelt University
Lawyer's Assistant Program
430 S. Michigan Avenue
Chicago, IL 60605

William Rainey Harper College
Legal Technology Program
Algonquin and Roselle Roads
Palatine, IL 60067

INDIANA
Indiana Central University
1400 E. Hanna Avenue
Indianapolis, IN 46227

University of Evansville
Legal Paraprofessional Pgms.

P.O. Box 329
Evansville, IN 47702

IOWA
Des Moines Area Cmty. College
2006 Ankeny Blvd.
Ankeny, IA 50021

Iowa Lakes Community College
826 N. 13th Street
Estherville, IA 51334

Marycrest College
1607 W. 12th Street
Davenport, IA 52804

KANSAS
Wichita State University
Legal Assistant Program
College of Business Administration
Wichita, KS 67208

Johnson County Cmty. College
Paralegal Program
College Blvd. at Quivera Road
Overland Park, KS 66210

KENTUCKY
Eastern Kentucky University
Lancaster Avenue
Richmond, KY 40475

Midway College
Midway, KY 40347

LOUISIANA
Louisiana State University in Shreveport
8515 Youree Drive
Shreveport, LA 71115

MARYLAND
Cmty. College of Baltimore
2901 Liberty Heights Ave.
Baltimore, MD 21215

Dundalk Cmty. College
7200 Sollers Point Road
Baltimore, MD 21222

Paralegal Institute (The)
914 Silver Spring Ave.
Suite 204
Silver Spring, MD 20910

University of Maryland
University College
College Park Campus
College Park, MD 20742

Villa Julie College
Legal Assistant Program
Greenspring Valley Road
Stevenson, MD 21153

Washington Business School
5454 Wisconsin Ave., N.W.
Chevy Chase, MD 20015

MASSACHUSETTS
Anna Maria College
Paralegal Program
Paxton, MA 01612

Bay Path Junior College
Legal Assistant Program
588 Longmeadow Street
Longmeadow, MA 01106

Bentley College
Inst. of Paralegal Studies
Beaver & Forest Streets
Waltham, MA 02154

Hampshire College
Amherst, MA 01002

Middlesex Cmty. College
Division of C.E.
Springs Road
Bedford, MA 01730

Univ. of Massachusetts-Boston
Ctr. for Legal Edtn. Services
100 Arlington Street
Boston, MA 02116

MICHIGAN
Baker Junior College of Bus.
1110 Eldon Baker Drive
Flint, MI 48507

Ferris State College
Big Rapids, MI 49307

Grand Valley State Colleges
School of Public Service
College Landing
467 Mackinac Hall
Allendale, MI 49401

Henry Ford Community College
5101 Evergreen Road
Dearborn, MI 48125

Hillsdale College
33 College Street
Hillsdale, MI 49242

Kellogg Community College
Battlecreek, MI

Lansing Community College
419 North Capitol
P.O. Box 40010
Lansing, MI 48901

Macomb County Cmty. College
South Campus
14500 Twelve Mile Road
Warren, MI 48093

Madonna College
26600 Schoolcraft Road
Livonia, MI 48150

Michigan Paraprofessional Training Institute, Inc.
1720 David Stott Bldg.
Detroit, MI 48226
     and
21700 Northwestern Highway
Ste. 515
Southfield, MI 48075

Mott Community College
1401 E. Court St.
Flint, MI 48503

Oakland University
Diploma Pgm. for Legal Assts.
Division of C. E.
Rochester, MI 48063

Washtenaw Community College
4800 East Huron River Drive
Ann Arbor, MI 48107

MINNESOTA
Inver Hills Community College
8445 College Trail
Inver Grove Heights, MN 55075

North Hennepin Cmty. College
7411 35th Avenue North
Minneapolis, MN 55445

University of Minnesota
General College
Legal Assistant Program
106 Nicholson Hall
Minneapolis, MN 55455

Winona State University
Paralegal Program
4330 W-7
Winona, MN 55987

MISSISSIPPI
Northwest Mississippi Jr. Clg.
300 North Panola Street
Senatobia, MS 38668

University of Mississippi
Paralegal Studies Program
Universities Center, Ste. 116
Jackson, MS 39211

Univ. of Southern Mississippi
P.O. Box 5267, Southern Station
Hattiesburg, MS 39401

MISSOURI
Avila College
11901 Wornall Road
Kansas City, MO 64145

Florissant Valley Cmty. College
3400 Perhall Road
St. Louis, MO 63135

Marysville College
13550 Conway Road
St. Louis, MO 63110

Missouri Western State College
4525 Downs Drive
St. Joseph, MO 64507

Penn Valley Cmty. College
Legal Technology Program
3201 S. W. Tfwy.
Kansas City, MO 64111

Rockhurst College
5225 Troost Avenue
Kansas City, MO 64110

Southeast Missouri State Univ.
Cape Girardeau, MO 63701

St. Louis Community College at Meramec
11333 Big Bend
St. Louis, MO 63122

Stephens College
Columbia, MO 65201

William Woods College
Paralegal Studies Program
Fulton, MO 63251

NEBRASKA
Lincoln School of Commerce
1821 K Street

P.O. Box 82826
Lincoln, NB 68501

Metropolitan City College
4469 Farham Street
Omaha, NB 68131

University of Nebraska
Omaha, NB 68132

NEVADA
Reno Junior College of Bus.
Wells & Wonder
Reno, NV 89502

NEW HAMPSHIRE
Rivier College
Nashua, NH

NEW JERSEY
Burlington County College
Pemberton-Brown Mills Road
Pemberton, NJ 08068

Cumberland County College
Legal Technology Program
P.O. Box 517
Vineland, NJ 08360

First School of Secretarial & Paralegal Studies
316 Main Street
East Orange, NJ 07018

Mercer County College
P.O. Box B
Trenton, NJ 08690

Middlesex County College
Legal Assistant Program
9 Ennis Drive
Hazlet, NJ 07730

Ocean County College
A.A.S. Legal Assistant
Toms River, NJ 08753

Plaza School (The)
Garden State Plaza
Rt. 17 & Rt. 4
Paramus, NJ 07652

Upsala College
Paralegal Program
Office of C.E. Beck 205
East Orange, NJ 07019

NEW MEXICO
Univ. of New Mexico Law School
1117 Stanford N.E.
Albuquerque, NM 87131

NEW YORK
Adelphi University
University College
Div. of Special Programs
Lawyer's Assistant Program
Garden City, L.I., NY 11530

Elizabeth Seton College
Legal Assistant Pgm.
1061 N. Broadway
Yonkers, NY 10701

Herkimer County Cmty. College
Herkimer, NY 13350

Hilbert College
5200 South Park Avenue
Hamburg, NY 14075

Junior College of Albany
140 New Scotland Avenue
Albany, NY 12208

Long Island University/APS
Paralegal Studies Program
Continuing Education, Rm. M101
LIU Brooklyn Center
Brooklyn, NY 11201

Long Island University
Greenvale, NY 11548

Marist College
North Road
Poughkeepsie, NY 12601

Nassau Community College
Paralegal Assistant Program
Stewart Avenue
Garden City, NY

New York University
Inst. of Paralegal Studies
School of C.E. in Law & Taxation
332 Shimkin Hall
50 West 4th Street
New York, NY 10003

Paralegal Institute
132 Nassau Street
New York, NY 10039

Schenectady County Cmty. Col.
Washington Avenue
Schenectady, NY 12305

Suffolk County Cmty. College
A.A.S. Paralegal Studies
533 College Road
Selden, NY 11784

NORTH CAROLINA
Central Carolina Tech. Inst.
Dept. of Community Colleges
1105 Kelly Drive
Sanford, NC 27330

Davidson County Cmty. College
P.O. Box 1287
Intersection of Old Greensboro Road & Interstate 40
Lexington, NC 27292

Fayetteville Technical Institute
P.O. Box 5236
Fayetteville, NC 28303

Greensboro College
Dept. of Business Administration
Greensboro, NC 27420

Pitt Technical Institute
Paralegal Program
P.O. Drawer 7007
Greenville, NC 27834

Southwestern Technical Institute
P.O. Box 95
Sylvia, NC 28779

OHIO
Capital University
2199 E. Main Street
Columbus, OH 43209

Dyke College
1375 E. 6th
Cleveland, OH 44114

Ohio Paralegal Institute
1001 Euclid Avenue
Suite 404
Cleveland, OH 44115

University of Toledo
Paralegal Program
Scott Park Campus
2501 Bancroft
Toledo, OH 43606

OKLAHOMA
Oscar Rose Junior College
Business Division
6420 Southeast 15th
Midwest City, OK 73110

Tulsa Junior College
Business Service Division
909 South Boston
Tulsa, OK 74119

University of Oklahoma
C.L.E. Law Center
Paralegal Program
300 Timberdell, Rm. 314
Norman, OK 73019

OREGON
Clackamas Community College
Business Education Department

19600 South Molalla Ave.
Oregon City, OR 97045

Lane Community College
Business Department
4000 E. 30th Avenue
Eugene, OR 97405

Mt. Hood Community College
26000 S.E. Stark Street
Gresham, OR 97030

Oregon State Dept. of Ed.
942 Lancaster Drive, N.E.
Salem, OR 97310

Portland Community College
12000 Southwest 49th Ave.
Portland, OR 97219

Rogue Community College
3345 Redwood Highway
Grants Pass, OR 97526

PENNSYLVANIA
Allegheny Community College
808 Ridge Avenue
Pittsburgh, PA 15212

Cedar Crest College
Legal Assistant Program
Allentown, PA 18104

Central Pennsylvania Bus. Schl.
College Hill Road
Summerdale, PA 17093

Gannon College
Perry Square
Erie, PA 16501

Harrisburg Area Cmty. College
3300 Cameron Street Road
Harrisburg, PA 17110

Inst. for Paralegal Tng. (The)
235 S. 17th St.
Philadelphia, PA 19103

Kings College
Wilkes Barre, PA 18711

Main Line Paralegal Institute
121 N. Wayne Avenue
Wayne, PA 19087

Northampton County Area Community College
Certificate Program
3835 Green Pond Road
Bethlehem, PA 18017

Widener College
Delaware County
Chester, PA 19013

SOUTH CAROLINA
Greenville Technical College
P.O. Box 5616 Station B
Greenville, SC 29606

Midlands Technical College
Drawer Q
Columbia, SC 29250

TENNESSEE
Cleveland State Cmty. College

Legal Assistant Program
P.O. Box 1205
Cleveland, TN 37311

University of Tennessee
Paralegal Training Program
Stokely Management Center (SMC) 608
Knoxville, TN 37916

TEXAS
Del Mar College
Legal Assistant Program
Baldwin & Ayers
Corpus Christi, TX 78404

El Centro College
Main and Lamar
Admissions Office
Dallas, TX 75202

Houston Community College System
Legal Assistant Program
4310 Dunlavy Avenue
Houston, TX 77006

Lamar University
Continuing Education
P.O. Box 10008
Beaumont, TX 77710

San Antonio College
San Antonio, TX 78212

Southwest Texas State Univ.
Lawyer's Assistant Program
Dept. of Political Science
San Marcos, TX 78666

Southwestern Paralegal Institute
999 One Main Plaza
Houston, TX 77002

Texas Para-Legal School-Conroe
c/o Extension Department
810 Main St., Ste. 203
Dallas, TX 75202

Texas Para-Legal School
608 Fannin, Ste. 1903
Houston, TX 77002

West Texas State University
School of Business
Dept. of Business Education & Office Education
Canyon, TX 79016

UTAH
University of Utah
Division of C.E.
Carlson Hall
Salt Lake City, UT 84112

Utah Technical College—Orem Campus
1200 South 800 West
Orem, UT 84057

VIRGINIA
Ferrum College
Ferrum, VA 24088

J. Sargeant Reynolds Cmty. Clg.
Parham Road Campus
P.O. Box 12084
Richmond, VA 23241

Tidewater Community College
1700 College Crescent
Virginia Beach, VA 23456

University College
Summer School/C.E.
University of Richmond
Richmond, VA 23173

Virginia Western Cmty. College
3095 Colonial Ave., S.W.
Roanoke, VA 24015

WASHINGTON
Bellevue Community College
Bellevue, WA 98007

Central Washington University
Program in Law & Justice
Ellensburg, WA 98926

City College
403–405 Lyon Bldg.
Seattle, WA 98104

Edmonds Community College
20000 68th Avenue West
Lynnwood, WA 98036

Fort Steilacoom Cmty. Clg.
9401 Farwest Drive SW
Tacoma, WA 98498

Highline Community College
Community College District #9
Midway, WA 98031

Spokane Community College
N. 1810 Greene St.
Spokane, WA 99207

WEST VIRGINIA
Marshall University Cmty. Clg.
Legal Assistant Program
Huntington, WV 25701

WISCONSIN
Lakeshore Technical Inst.
1290 North Avenue
Cleveland, WI 53015

Code of Ethics and Professional Responsibility of the National Association of Legal Assistants, Inc.

Preamble

It is the responsibility of every legal assistant to adhere strictly to the accepted standards of legal ethics and to live by general principles of proper conduct. The performance of the duties of the legal assistant shall be governed by specific canons as defined herein in order that justice will be served and the goals of the profession attained.

The canons of ethics set forth hereafter are adopted by the National Association of Legal Assistants, Inc., as a general guide, and the enumeration of these rules does not mean there are not others of equal importance although not specifically mentioned.

Canon 1. A legal assistant shall not perform any of the duties that lawyers only may perform nor do things that lawyers themselves may not do.

Canon 2. A legal assistant may perform any task delegated and supervised by a lawyer so long as the lawyer is responsible to the client, maintains a direct relationship with the client, and assumes full professional responsibility for the work product.

Canon 3. A legal assistant shall not engage in the practice of law by giving legal advice, appearing in court, setting fees, or accepting cases.

Canon 4. A legal assistant shall not act in matters involving professional legal judgment as the services of a lawyer are essential in the public interest whenever the exercise of such judgment is required.

Canon 5. A legal assistant must act prudently in determining the extent to which a client may be assisted without the presence of a lawyer.

Canon 6. A legal assistant shall not engage in the unauthorized practice of law and shall assist in preventing the unauthorized practice of law.

Canon 7. A legal assistant must protect the confidences of a client, and it shall be unethical for a legal assistant to violate any statute now in effect or hereafter to be enacted controlling privileged communications.

Canon 8. It is the obligation of the legal assistant to avoid conduct which would cause the lawyer to be unethical or even appear to be unethical, and loyalty to the employer is incumbent upon the legal assistant.

Canon 9. A legal assistant shall work continually to maintain integrity and a high degree of competency throughout the legal profession.

Canon 10. A legal assistant shall strive for perfection through education in order to better assist the legal profession in fulfilling its duty of making legal services available to clients and the public.

Canon 11. A legal assistant shall do all other things incidental, necessary, or expedient for the attainment of the ethics and responsibilities imposed by statute or rule of court.

Canon 12. A legal assistant is governed by the American Bar Association Code of Professional Responsibility.

Adopted May 1, 1975

Code of Professional Responsibility
of the American Bar Association

Canon 1. A LAWYER SHOULD ASSIST IN MAINTAINING THE INTEGRITY AND COMPETENCE OF THE LEGAL PROFESSION.

Canon 2. A LAWYER SHOULD ASSIST THE LEGAL PROFESSION IN FULFILLING ITS DUTY TO MAKE LEGAL COUNSEL AVAILABLE.

Canon 3. A LAWYER SHOULD ASSIST IN PREVENTING THE UNAUTHORIZED PRACTICE OF LAW.

Canon 4. A LAWYER SHOULD PRESERVE THE CONFIDENCES AND SECRETS OF A CLIENT.

Canon 5. A LAWYER SHOULD EXERCISE INDEPENDENT PROFESSIONAL JUDGMENT ON BEHALF OF A CLIENT.

Canon 6. A LAWYER SHOULD REPRESENT A CLIENT COMPETENTLY.

Canon 7. A LAWYER SHOULD REPRESENT A CLIENT ZEALOUSLY WITHIN THE BOUNDS OF THE LAW.

Canon 8. A LAWYER SHOULD ASSIST IN IMPROVING THE LEGAL SYSTEM.

Canon 9. A LAWYER SHOULD AVOID EVEN THE APPEARANCE OF PROFESSIONAL IMPROPRIETY.

Affirmation of Responsibility of the National Federation of Paralegal Associations

Preamble

The paralegal profession is committed to responsibility to the individual citizen and the public interest. In reexamining contemporary institutions and systems and in questioning the relationship of the individual to the law, members of the paralegal profession recognize that a redefinition of the traditional delivery of legal services is essential in order to meet the expressed needs of the general public.

This Affirmation of Responsibility asserts that the principles recognized by the National Federation of Paralegal Associations are essential to the continuing work of the paralegal.

Through this Affirmation of Responsibility, the National Federation of Paralegal Associations recognizes the responsibility placed upon each paralegal and encourages the dedication of the paralegal to the development of the profession.

I. Professional Responsibility

The paralegal is dedicated to the development of the paralegal profession and endeavors to expand the responsibilities and the scope of paralegal work.

Discussion: There is room for a great deal of growth in the paralegal profession and an opportunity to tap human resources to assist an overburdened legal system. This Affirmation of Responsibility aims to establish a positive attitude through which the paralegal may perceive the importance, responsibility and potential of the paralegal profession and work toward enhancing its professional status.

II. *The Role of the Paralegal and the Unauthorized Practice of Law*

The paralegal performs all functions permitted under law which are not in violation of the unauthorized practice of law statutes within the applicable jurisdiction.

Discussion: The increase in the number of paralegals has given rise to much discussion concerning what the paralegal may or may not do. This development has prompted new interpretations as to what constitutes the practice of law, and thus it is unwise to delineate exactly or to restrict the types of tasks which the paralegal may perform.

However, this Affirmation of Responsibility insists on compliance with regulations governing the practice of law as determined by the applicable jurisdiction. It is not within the scope of the Affirmation of Responsibility to change or challenge any of these statutes.

Whenever the paralegal performs tasks related to the delivery of legal services, it is the responsibility of the paralegal to insure that the applicable unauthorized practice of law statutes are not violated and that the best interests of the public are met. To this end, it is the responsibility of the paralegal to be aware of legislation affecting the paralegal profession and the legal welfare of the public.

III. *Competence and Education*

The paralegal maintains integrity and promotes competence through continuing education.

Discussion: The growth of a profession and the attainment and maintenance of individual competence require an ongoing incorporation of new concepts and techniques. Continuing education enables the paralegal to become aware of new developments in the field of law and provides the opportunity to improve skills used in the delivery of legal services.

The paralegal recognizes the importance of maintaining an interest in the development of continuing paralegal education. Professional competence is each paralegal's responsibility. The exchange of ideas and skills benefits the profession, the legal community, and the general public.

IV. Client Confidences

The paralegal is responsible for maintaining all client confidences.

Discussion: The paralegal is aware of the importance of preserving all client confidences. Such information is understood to be a vital part of the relationship between the paralegal and the client, facilitating the delivery of legal services. The confidentiality of this information is respected at all times.

V. Protection of the Public Interest

The paralegal upholds the responsibility of protecting public interests by contributing to the delivery of quality legal services and by maintaining a sensitivity to public needs.

Discussion: The paralegal should make every effort to educate the public as to the services and tasks that paralegals may render. Such services may be performed within the setting of a law firm, public agency, governmental agency, business or within a defined program specifically addressing the needs of increased legal services to the public, including *pro bono* work.

The paralegal should inform the public of the scope of duties that the paralegal may perform and should encourage the public to examine issues and to explore innovative means by which an increased availability of moderate cost legal services may be obtained. It is also within the responsibility of the paralegal to maintain an interest in the development and continuation of paralegal education programs that address the public interest.

VI. Support of Professional Association

The paralegal recognizes the necessity of membership and participation in the professional association.

Discussion: One of the hallmarks of any profession is its professional association, founded for the purpose, among many others, of determining standards and guidelines for the growth and development of the profession. The paralegal profession is in a dynamic stage of growth. The ability of individual paralegals to determine the direction and quality of that growth depends largely upon the success of the paralegal association in providing effective representation of and communication among members of the profession. Through the professional association, the paralegal is able to promote a cooperative effort with members of the legal community, paralegal educators and the general public to improve the quality of paralegal participation in the delivery of legal services.

The role which the paralegal occupies in the legal system is, to some extent, the result of the cumulative and cooperative efforts of paralegals working through the paralegal association. The continued and increased contribution of paralegals to the delivery of legal services is dependent upon a further delineation of their skills, qualifications and areas of responsibility. It is, therefore, incumbent upon each paralegal to promote the growth of the profession through support of and participation in the endeavors of the paralegal association.